ACTS OF
SUBVERSION

A Paperback Original
First published 1991 by
Poolbeg Press Ltd
Knocksedan House,
Swords, Co Dublin, Ireland

Poolbeg Press receives financial assistance from the Arts
Council/An Chomhairle Ealaíon, Ireland

ISBN 1 85371 124 1

Cover photograph and design by Gillian Buckley
Set by Richard Parfrey in ITC Stone 10/15
Printed by The Guernsey Press Ltd,
Vale, Guernsey, Channel Islands

ACTS OF SUBVERSION

LIZ McMANUS
POOLBEG

To John

ONE

Galway, 1972

Waiting was the worst, Oran thought, anything was better than waiting. He leant forward and gnawed on his knuckles. Like an unrolled bolt of cloth, the grassy expanse of Eyre Square stretched out before him. At one corner, Shop Street opened the way to his destination. Oran chose to ignore it. As the sky changed colour and evening shadows chased across the pavement he sat on, hunched over on the park bench. Waiting.

A church bell chimed. Time to go. Oran stood up. Not too fast and not too slow, he reminded himself, as he loped across the grass. In the mouth of Shop Street he was conscious of passers-by flitting past him like moths in the gathering dusk but none of them wasted a second glance on the slight, long-haired boy in jeans. In the city of Galway he was just another student setting out for a night on the tear or on a date with some girl. It was an anonymity that Oran took comfort in.

A sudden outburst of lights and rich garlicky smells caught him by surprise. He hadn't noticed the restaurant set back from the pavement, one of the expensive kind with tinted windows and heavy curtains and a hand-written menu in French displayed in a glass case outside. It was so discreet that when the doors of the restaurant opened, Oran panicked momentarily. A middle-aged couple emerged and stopped on the pavement. The man put his arm around the woman and she rubbed up close to him, laughing a responsive, well-fed laugh. She was tanned and fleshy and wore high-heeled sandals with thongs of gold that squeezed her ankles. From the interior of the restaurant a fragment of piano music escaped into the street. The couple moved off, arm-in-arm. In their wake, the smells of her perfume and of expensive cooking lingered like the vaguest of memories. Then the doors swung to, shutting Oran out.

He was distracted by this casual invasion of his senses. The whiff of opulence reminded him of Garret Heaney and Jane O'Molloy. *Only the best of eating and drinking and keeping the builder's wife satisfied...*Maybe the two of them were inside that restaurant now, drunk on love and wine and a good dinner while outside, in the deepening shadows, Oran kept walking and tried to get a grip on the anxiety rolling around in his guts.

He would have felt better if he had something else to distract him. Something weighty and solid to hold on to while he was tracking his way through the streets in the direction of the bridge and beyond it, towards the barred gates of the factory. Something substantial like a gun. Yes. Right now, he would have felt better with a gun burning a hole in his pocket than the way he felt, defenceless and surviving on his wits and hungry. Very hungry, all of a sudden, at the thought of Garret Heaney stuffing his face across some candle-lit table, his mouth watering with anticipation at what was for afters.

Well, that makes two of us with something to look forward to, Oran grinned briefly into the twilight. Wherever you are, Mr Garret Heaney, you've forgotten one thing. *Beware...*

A car slid along the street, a shabby blue Cortina. Oran held his breath as he watched for a familiar face but the car passed him by, driven by a woman he had never seen before. He straightened up, liberated by the sight of the receding car tail-lights. Resolution filled the hollow space inside him. Without realising it, he quickened his pace and the drumming of his shoes on the pavement told him that there was no going back. So this is it, he thought and, clutching at air inside his pockets, he cut his way through the heart of the city.

Like an expectant woman, the city of Galway, usually misty and wet as a swamp, brightened around him, its pale walls blushing in the glow of sunset. This is how he had imagined Galway once, a blurred impression of lichened stone buildings and seagulls wheeling above a river.

Flame-coloured clouds piled up behind the roofs of Nun's Island. The buildings sharpened into focus against the fading light. This was a scene from his imagination all right, a postcard version of the city, pink and picturesque, nothing like the dank, dilapidated world that had greeted him when he stepped off the train and had seen Galway for the first time. To Oran's eyes, accustomed to the metropolitan skyline of Dublin, the sight of Galway had been melancholy; a squat settlement straggling around the bay, water seeping along its canals and the River Corrib gushing out of the confines of the city. As the train approached the station, images had flashed up beyond the windows. At the edge of the city, new metal-clad factories and suburban houses sprouted out of bare fields. Then a change of direction produced a tidal inlet of grey sand and seaweed before he was delivered among the fortifications of stone and weathered bridges. Rain had fallen that October morning with an intensity that Oran had presumed would last five or ten minutes. In Galway he learnt that a fall of rain could last a season.

Its centre was a mosaic of narrow streets. Alien unnerving territory. Old crones wrapped in black or dun-coloured shawls flapped past him. In the tourist shops, shillelaghs nestled malevolently among lengths of tweed. Outside the gates of the cathedral, bony-faced men and women from Connemara set up their stalls and sold duck-eggs and carrots and live chickens squashed into cages. He had expected somewhere less foreign, less imbued with its own native individuality.

He was drawn towards the docks, to where fishing trawlers jostled for space with Scandinavian timber-boats and the lock-gates opened out to the reaches of the bay. The sea, at least, was familiar; the sea was the same anywhere. He took refuge in a dockside pub and sat down at the corner of the bar, beside a sweet-smelling turf fire and yet, even into that haven, Galway pursued him. Soon after he sat down, a group of men came into the pub. Big men speaking Irish, Aran islanders gathered in to swop news of home. Courteously they nodded at him and then turned away to talk among themselves but Oran was not reassured. He drained his glass and hurried out, fearful that the men might attempt to strike up a conversation with him in a language that bore no relation to the dead phrases that he had been taught to learn, parrot-fashion, at school.

TWO

"What's this I hear?"

"What, Da?"

Fourteen-year-old Oran was deceived by the restrained tone of his father's question. Then he saw his father's nostrils dilate. It was like looking at something under water, seeing only a surface disturbance and trying to judge from it the size and identity of its source.

"You're not working."

Silence.

"So the Brothers tell me."

Them and him. It was a conspiracy.

"I do enough."

"That's not what I hear." His father's face was growing puffy with anger. "You young pup, take that smirk off your face."

"Look, I'll show you." Oran emptied his satchel on to the table. His father looked at the books spilled out on the oilcloth. Oran knew he had him. "See Da?" he said. "That's my maths book. You know, my geometric and algebraic tables and that's my trigonometry."

His father picked up a book. His hands looked

enormous, their knobbled joints ingrained with coal-dust that no amount of washing could remove. Oran jabbered, filling him up with nonsense, stringing theorems together, reciting bits of his Latin grammar. All the time he was speaking, his father gripped the textbook in his hands, bending the spine until it began to shear apart. Oran reached out to take back the book.

"See, Da?" he said. "The Brothers are never satisfied."

His father lifted another book. *Pride and Prejudice*.

"I'm finished with that one." Not a trace of sarcasm in Oran's voice. "D'you want to read it, Da?"

Impossible to tell how well he knew his father and his stumbling efforts to read even the simplest headline in a newspaper. Usually his father covered up his inability to read by evincing a lack of interest, as he did then, throwing aside the book and staring miserably into his hands. But Oran knew that, deep down, his father was afraid of the Brothers. Not like Oran. Living with his father had given him an edge when it came to shrugging off the systematic temper of the classroom strap.

A trivial incident, a spilt cup or a torn paper, was enough to start an avalanche of retribution, his father's fists flailing around the kitchen table, battering at any young head that didn't duck in time. There were night-time echoes too, that travelled down the channels of Oran's childhood, so incomprehensible that he could never be sure if they were real or imagined; hard bestial noises that cracked and shuddered through the fabric of the house.

Oran had been the child that his parents had waited for. Three sisters had been born before him, loved for their own sakes but not prized the way that a son is. Throughout his childhood a protective ring of female heads encircled Oran.

"That boy," said his maternal grandmother who had made, for his christening, the long journey from County Fermanagh to the red-brick terraced house in Ringsend, "has been born with the head of a bishop."

"Away out of that," his father had cried out above the laughter. "Oran Reidy will haul coal the same as his father does and the same as *his* father did before him."

As Oran grew, so did the network of densely-packed streets around him. Penrose Street, Hanover Square, Vavasour…Thorncastle…South Lotts Road. When he was old enough Oran was taken by his father on his coal round and the tock-tock of the horse's hooves served as an accompaniment to the tum-te-tum litany of places already singing inside the boy's head. Irish Meatpackers. Boland's Mills. The Yacht Bar. The Irish Glass Bottle Company…

Industrial continents loomed out of an ocean of terraced houses. Further out where the Pigeon House

Road tongued into the sea, the air was lazy with the call of seagulls. There, toy ships hovered on the horizon before they dropped off the edge of the world.

In Fenian Street there was a different landscape. Cavernous buildings, wearing an air of frantic instability, were full of noise and filth and broken glass and children. Stealthily roof slates slid into the street and narrowly missed killing someone. Timber trusses uncoupled, ceilings sagged and blossomed green mould, window-frames rotted to spongy splinters, doors yawned off their hinges.

On the doorsteps Oran watched, intrigued, while his father played a part. His face creased into a grin of self-loathing, Billy Reidy winked at the women in their cheap, patterned aprons, nudging them into paying what they owed, easing coins out of their pockets.

"I haven't a shilling," sighed a handsome woman with eyes the colour of peppermint.

"Ah mam, a fine woman like yourself."

She laughed. Her hearty laugh made Oran want to laugh too. She touched his upturned face with her fingers.

"Would you take it in kind?" One hand on her hip she thrust out her breasts. Her expression was insistent. Enigmatic. Her fingers abandoned Oran's face and wandered instead along the edge of his father's belt.

"Wouldya?" she persisted, her green eyes

darkening. Oran's father wrenched her hand away. He must have hurt her, Oran thought sadly as he watched the woman's face redden. He wanted to hear her laugh and to feel the rough pads of her fingers on his cheek.

"Cow-all..." His father took up the familiar yodel as he climbed back on to the dray. Unexpectedly he added, "Cow-all for moneeee..." and winked at Oran.

And Oran was too abashed to ask him why.

At home his father withdrew like a crab into a shell. There was a place carved out for him in an armchair beside the fire and he sat there for hours, poring over copybooks into which he scrawled his accounts. On Saturday evenings, when the curtains were drawn and the fire crackled in the grate, he served them up a concoction of his own making: a mixture of onions and slices of bread and gravy that the children lapped up hungrily while, above their heads, their father's face rose, flushed and happy, round as a harvest moon.

His mother was different. Like Oran she was pale-skinned and slightly built and her movements were delicate and quick. She sang a lot and her voice retained its Northern lilt despite the years of living in Dublin.

Her mysteries were penetrable, to be shared by her children.

"Where are you going?" his father wanted to know.

"You know well where I'm going." Her voice was

gentle, the barb hidden in the words.

"Mixing with corner-boys, I suppose. A fine example to be giving the lad."

"He could always stay."

Oran, pulling on his coat, didn't like the sound of that and he clutched at his mother's hand. Reassuringly, she squeezed his fingers.

"I know what you're after," his father grumbled. "Am I here to wipe his backside? Out working day and night and this is the thanks I get. You gallivanting in the streets and making a holy show of yourself."

"Billy, the men have died. Would you deny me the chance to honour them?"

He snorted in disgust. "There'll be no honour in that O'Connell Street crowd." Then, troubled, he peered at her. "Nell, there could be trouble down there with them latchicos. You wouldn't be up to them."

She smiled into the mirror as she tied her headscarf under her chin.

"Don't be an oul' fool. I'm a grown woman."

"And one with no sense, taking a child out into a street brawl. Ye'll end up in jail, the two of ye."

His voice rose. He was only getting into his stride when she took Oran's hand again and led him firmly to the front door.

"Will I bring you home a bag of chips?"

Her question dangled in the air. The room was unusually quiet, the wireless switched off, the only sound was the ticking of the clock and the coals breaking in the grate. His father stood up and, instead of replying, he turned to face the wall. For a moment she faltered, her hand on the latch as a goodbye trailed uncertainly from her lips.

"I'll bring you back a bag of chips," she decided. There was no response. She rallied and carefully picked the rim of her scarf up over the crown of her head and, grasping Oran's hand, she let herself out of the house. Once they were in the street she breathed deeply and let out a giggle, "Gee-up, Oran, or we'll miss it."

The wind whipped across their faces as they hurried towards the end of the terraced street. Behind them, the front door banged open and they saw him standing, black and angry, against the light spilling into the street. He bellowed like a wounded beast, feeding the neighbours with gossip. Loud and unrestrained, his farewell blew the pair of them around the corner.

"Why don't youse..." he paused for breath and then, bitterly, "why don't youse bring me back a bag of *poison*?"

Purposefully his mother led Oran along the city streets. By the time they turned into O'Connell Street, his legs had grown heavy. Crowds of people were gathered around Nelson's Pillar and they pressed in on all sides. The proximity of their bodies and the rough texture of their coats grazing his cheeks confused Oran and he shouted out with fear. But his cry was lost in the roar of thousands of voices. Up high, from a vantage point that he couldn't see, someone else had captured his mother's attention. Transfixed, she gazed upwards while Oran tugged frantically at her coat and blubbered. At last she heard him and bent down to lift him up in her arms.

"Listen to the speech that man is making, Oran," she said. Her face was radiant. "It's about two men, about two heroes that died for Ireland!"

Obediently he strained to hear. The distant babble meant nothing to him and he reached out to pat his mother's face, trying to regain her attention. Her grip on him tightened and he was comforted by the warmth of her arms around him but her eyes still hungered for something beyond his comprehension. When he lifted his finger to his mouth he discovered to his surprise, that it was wet and tasted of salt. The noise of the crowd welled up around him. "South and O'Hanlon...South and O'Hanlon..."The chant reverberated through his body. It was a rhythm that frightened him when it issued, alien and unbidden, out of his mother's mouth.

"Mammy!" he wailed, "I want to go home."

Again his cry was swallowed up by the crowd. Defeated, he slumped in his mother's arms while she continued to stand, erect and proud, until all the speeches were ended and the rosary recited and the snow began to fall.

Coming home, the alternation of light and darkness distracted him. Fragments pattered down on his clothes and caught in his lashes, causing him to blink. His mother's hand was warm and steady in this new fantastic world of snowflakes pouring through the yellow beams of streetlights. The pavements were transformed into a new substance, dry and crumbling, that muffled the sound of his foorsteps as the whirling flakes blurred his vision. In later life, whenever snow fell, Oran was reminded of that night when he walked with his mother through the streets of Dublin and she sang songs that made him think of Christmas. The same tunes that, her face ablaze from the heat of the fire and the glass of port taken to give her courage, Nellie would stand up in the parlour and sing in her true, sweet voice to honour, she said, "the men of 1916 and the bould James Connollee."

As a schoolboy, Oran ran messages for his mother. When Mr Sharpe, the carpenter who had his workshop at the end of the street, was taken away by the Guards in the middle of the night, Oran understood. Every day, after school, he walked through the dark workshop—a mute witness now to its owner's disappearance—carrying little parcels despatched by his mother to help Mrs Sharpe in her trouble. On Easter morning he and Nellie flaunted little green, white and orange lilies on their lapels that they got for pennies outside the church after mass from a grey-looking man with a squint who wasn't quite right in the head.

"*Beir bua*," Oran's mother always said when she took the lilies. And the man's wild agitated response used to send Oran into fits of giggles. *Beirbuabeirbuabeirbuabeirbua...*

As the streets of Galway opened out to a watery vista, something in the sound of the River Corrib somersaulting over the weir caught his attention. A rumbling echo. *Beir bua*, thought Oran, *beirbuabeirbua*. And he kept walking not too fast, not too slow, towards his destination.

THREE

On Nun's Island, in the middle of Galway, stood the factory, HEANEY spelt out in tall black letters over the gates. It was a hotch-potch of old buildings, stone walls and modern corrugated asbestos sheeting. Oran felt that the factory was anticipating his every move. As if it were lying in wait. Nerves, he thought but, all the same, he kept close to the balustrade of the bridge, not too fast and not too slow, and at last, he was free to slip into the laneway that skirted the perimeter of the building. On either side, walls reared up to enclose him and somewhere above his head, a bird sang.

A new sound underscored the birdsong; a steady rhythm that shuddered up from the bedrock of limestone. Hearing it, Oran was filled with an irrational anger.

"Jesus Christ!" he wanted to shout. "Wait for me!"

Somewhere up ahead, he knew, the truck was inching its way up the laneway.

That hidden tailboard was a relic from his past, from a time when horse and dray had been abandoned. In their place, an open-back truck gave his father an urgency to press on, regardless. And

Oran, old enough now to make deliveries, could find himself being left behind on the street.

"Jesus Christ, wait for me!"

A mistake, of course. And he knew it as soon as the words were out of his mouth. His father came up close, trenches of anger dug out of his face.

"You young pup. You don't know..." his voice thickening, "good food on the table and clothes on your back. When I think how lucky you are...and an education." His hand curled with a venom that made Oran stagger. At that moment something rose inside Oran. Something clear-cut and hard and ugly. He could picture them both as tiny figures hemmed in by the terraced houses; the movement of their feet as they traded punches; the blood trickling down his father's face.

There they stood, caught in an impasse, his father facing into decline and he on the ascendant. The law of the jungle was on Oran's side but it failed to dampen down the fear that assailed him, filling his mouth with its dry, debilitating taste. It was safer to resort to words, his old weapon against his father.

"Come on, you ignorant old man, come on and get me!" Oran danced around him, shouting hysterically. "Humping coal like a donkey. It's all you're good for."

Net curtains twitched up and down the street. *Ignorant*. That got to him. Bull's-eye. He turned his back on Oran and smashed his fists down on the mudguard of the truck. Oran was afraid for him then, and afraid of the coldness seeping between his father's hunched shoulders.

"What's going on?" A tall red-haired woman stood at a doorway, uncritical and curious. Without a word, his father climbed back into the truck and revved it fast so that Oran had to run to catch up. Oran was sick of it all, sick of his father and sick of the poverty on the doorstep, the endless round of women, thin and worn-out or obese and slovenly, whingeing and cajoling a week's grace. He wanted to be rid of the tenements with their chopped-up rooms and gouged-out fanlights, their smashed windows and graffiti, the children who hurled stones and meaningless abuse after them as they went on their rounds.

One person he liked was Mrs Gaughan.

Where other people had arms and legs, Mrs Gaughan had limbs like grotesque sticks. An invalid, she spent her days in a low-ceilinged attic room in Fenian Street and the sight of her trapped in that narrow dark space made Oran think of an injured spider hiding in the eaves. Around her were piled up the belongings of a lifetime packed into plastic bags. The mantelpiece overflowed with her treasures; a bottle of Lourdes water; the crowned and skirted figure of the Infant of Prague; assorted crucifixes and ornaments; an ashtray with *A Present From Liverpool* printed on it.

"There you are, son." A crooked smile accompanied Mrs Gaughan's greeting. "Come in and make yourself a cup of tea."

Once he had boiled up a pot, Oran descended the rickety stairs, trying not to slop hot tea on his wrists and raised, two-handed, the cup to be consecrated by the satisfied smacking of his father's lips and the inevitable benediction, "Thank God for your strength, Oran. That poor sick woman suffers every minute of her life and offers it up cheerfully. It's little enough you have to put up with."

Sometimes when Oran, bent under a sack of coal, arrived at the top of the stairs, he found the Legion woman was already there ahead of him. The Legion woman came once a week to tend to Mrs Gaughan's needs. She took no notice of Oran as she draped a sheet between the bedposts to form a makeshift screen and then went into the kitchen to fill up a basin with hot water from the kettle.

"Don't go away, son." Mrs Gaughan strained to catch sight of him. "We'll be ready in a mo."

On these occasions her expression was complicit. Mrs Gaughan suffered visitations from the Legion of Mary because she was in no position to dispense with their services but, after their departure, her mouth would screw up in disgust. *"Holy Joes!"* and then she would bless herself.

After Oran had refilled the kettle and set it on the gas-ring he sat on the edge of his chair waiting for the

Legion woman to leave. He enjoyed being with Mrs Gaughan. She had a simple gaiety and asked him questions about himself and seemed to find his answers absorbing. He was content to wait, listening to the sound of the sponge sloshing quietly over her wasted skin.

Once, without warning, the sheet slipped and her naked body lay exposed to his pop-eyed stare. Her swollen, shiny-skinned knees were bent up to frame the opening between her legs and he saw her other mouth, in its perpetual O, mirroring his astonishment. Her venus mount was bony and hairless. White as marble. And yet, between her skinny thighs as if a knife had broken the skin of a plum, there was a slit through which the insides of Mrs Gaughan throbbed lasciviously at him.

The low room brimmed with female flesh. The arms of the Legion woman swelled out of her cardigan, her massive breasts threatening to erupt shamelessly, as the buttons of her crimplene overall ached under the strain of her every movement. Unaware of his discomfiture, the Legion woman pulled the nightdress over Mrs Gaughan's head and lifted her up into a sitting position. Once she had her rosary-beads threaded between her fingers, Mrs Gaughan was ready to face another day, jammed in her nest of pillows and staring into space.

"Can't you hear the kettle, son?" she asked. Oran, his face burning and his cock bulging, stumbled into the kitchen and stood, appalled, in front of the gas-ring, while the air filled up with steam. He became aware of someone standing beside him.

"Ya feckin' eejit." Casually the Legion woman stretched past him to turn off the gas. Her body was so close to him that his nostrils filled with the pungency of her sweat. "D'you want to burn a hole in it or what?" Her expression slackened and she displayed her tongue, pink and quivering, within the lipsticked margins of her mouth.

From the bedroom Mrs Gaughan's voice came, thin and urgent. "Come here to me, darling," she entreated him but Oran couldn't. Trapped between her sick scrawniness and the steaming corpulence of the Legion woman he felt the breath was being squeezed out of his body. He made his escape, rushing past them both and plunging out the door.

Ever consider Uni?" One of the Brothers asked. "They have grants now to help boys like you."

Surprised, Oran found a door opening and a route unravelling in front of him when he least expected it. He was lucky all right. When he told his parents they stared at him, mesmerised. A son at university... who would have dreamt? The wonder of it rolled around inside their mouths like butter. Money would be found. He could see their minds working in consort, their reverence for education outweighing any other consideration. Even he felt awe at the measure of his victory.

All the same, he wondered in alarm when he opened up the letter with its official seal. University College, Galway! He hadn't even known that Galway had a university. The Brother had arranged everything and Oran hadn't questioned his judgement. Uni was Uni, no matter what, the Brother said, and Oran was in no position to be choosy about which university he'd end up in. Take what he could get, the Brother said.

All the same, Oran thought.

"You have been accepted for a place in the Faculty of Arts..."Instantly the ramshackle familiarity of home and the streets around him rose in his estimation. Galway, the land of red petticoats and Padraig Pearse and pampooties. He stared down at the letter while his mother moved around him, preparing the dinner. He was soothed by the precision of her hands as she pressed out the creases on the oilcloth and laid out knives and forks that she had laid out a thousand times before. His baby spoon was caught up in the cutlery like a miniature *memento mori*, his initials engraved on its thin, curved handle.

"Look at that," she said, smiling quietly. The spoon looked so vulnerable, lying in the hollow of his mother's palm. Oran felt responsible for the leanness of her arm, the chapped tissuey texture of her skin, as if he had grown strong at her expense. He flattened out the letter to show her.

"Ach, my Gawd!" In times of excitement the Northern inflection in her voice became more marked. For a moment she was speechless and then, throwing open the kitchen window, she shouted across the yard, "Billy Reidy, come out right away!"

Slowly the door of the lean-to shed eased open. His father stepped out, his eyes narrowing against the bright sunlight.

"I'm not deaf, woman."

"Billy!" Her cry leapt out across the blackened space and the weight of coal heaped along the walls.

"Well?" He stood in the yard and looked at her.

"He has his place got at college!" It was a shout of triumph.

An expression flitted across his father's face. Of wonder or pride or envy, it was impossible to tell. He said nothing.

"Ach, Billy!" she cried.

He smiled bleakly at her. "And you want all the neighbours to hear about it?" But his voice was light, ironic, the harshness gone out of it. Satisfied, she banged the window shut.

"He's as pleased as I am," she crowed at Oran, "even if he does act the anti-Christ."

Her arms around him and the salty taste of her tears reminded him of the night she had carried him and how she had wept for Seán South. Now she couldn't rest and, like a trapped bird, she fluttered around the kitchen. Oran sat down. He felt deflated, as if he had scored an own-goal. His mother's delight mocked him and it was a relief when his father opened the back door and stepped up into the kitchen. With studied indifference his father turned on the tap and washed his hands. After drying his hands he sat down at the table.

"Well, do we still eat or not?" he asked.

She was oblivious to them both. Madly she stirred saucepans and banged plates down before them. Unable to contain her joy any longer she opened her mouth and began to sing. Strains of "The Galway Shawl" rose above the plumping of potatoes on the stove. In unspoken accord father and son dived for cover. They split the evening paper between them and burrowed behind barricades of newsprint in order to read with fierce concentration about "The Favourite That Was Left Behind at the Curragh."

FOUR

A round the corner the laneway widened at the
rear of the factory. By the time Oran reached it,
the truck carrying the three men had come to a halt
outside the gates. In the passenger-seat, Dominick
Keegan was talking, his head pulling from side to
side in a frenzy of anxiety. Beside him, his companion
looked like a lugubrious sheepdog, a dark shaggy
mound of a man propped up at the driving-wheel, a
sparkle of spit at the side of his mouth. And squashed
against the passenger door, Kevin, the schoolboy, was
giggling with fright.

For a moment nothing happened. Then the door
opened and Kevin unfolded his tall ungainly body in
order to step on to the ground. Dominick closed the
door after him and rolled down the window.
Wordlessly, he nodded at Oran. While the two boys
pulled on their balaclavas, the older man leant out to
speak to the schoolboy, repeating instructions that
they knew by heart. Oran felt a spurt of resentment.
To Kevin, he thought, and not to me.

"Make sure, you're not seen."

"OK."

"Remember, take as much as you can."

"Yeah."

"And for Jesus sake, remember…"

"Yeah, OK."

The gates that led into the rear of the factory were old and rusty, patched up with bits of sheeting and barbed wire. When he touched the lock, it broke apart easily in Oran's hands.

"Jeez!" breathed Kevin in his ear, "some people just ask to be robbed."

Yes, Oran agreed silently, setting the balance right, that's all we're doing. You've been at it for years, Garret Heaney, robbing the people blind. Now you'll know what it feels like to be on the other side. *Beware…*

"Are you coming?" Kevin muttered hoarsely. His eyes were distraught inside their black woollen rims. He jerked his head in the direction of the factory but he didn't move. Instead, he waited for Oran to take the first step. At that moment, Oran was aware that their roles were being reversed. Now, rather than leading the way, the schoolboy Kevin was following him, although he did so reluctantly, like a tall unhappy shadow, unable to stop himself.

Oran pushed open the gates and walked into the yard.

FIVE

Jane O'Molloy was not, as Oran had imagined, eating dinner in a good restaurant and getting drunk on love with Garret Heaney. Around her, domestic objects impeded her progress, a tricycle in the hall, a pile of laundry on the stairs. She dithered over the children's anoraks, her mind preoccupied by threats in the air. Threats and promises. And, like Oran, she was waiting.

"Aren't you coming to visit Granny with us?" Was he bewitched, she wondered, this little boy who knew how to manufacture guilt in her so effortlessly?

"Not today, darling." She opened the front door to let the children out. Leaning against a pilaster she watched as they ran down the steps and out across the lawn that curved under the trees. The evening air was fresh with the smell of newly-cut grass.

In an instant a tableau formed—of two tall, long-limbed, sandy-coloured figures, the man with a shock of carroty hair and she, the paler version of the pair. They could have been brother and sister, born out of the same stock. Mr and Mrs O'Molloy with their two children on the steps of their house. It was a scene made familiar by earlier illustrations, portraits hung in gilt frames, of people of substance. Defining property relations as love, honour, and obedience. The setting was right, the fine Georgian house at Bearna, just recently come on the market and sold for an undisclosed sum, an unusual property for the area, the dream-child of an eccentric eighteenth-century landowner out to prove that civilisation could be made to extend anywhere, even into a Connacht wilderness. A house that had been sensitively renovated by its new owners although, as Jane was fond of saying, it will take twenty years before it's right.

In the original tableau, there would have been servants, holding a horse's bridle or ramrod straight in the seat of a carriage. Now there was only the au pair, skulking by the car, resentful about being dislodged from her cosy niche at the television. But Jane had insisted. You will go, Monique, because I say so!

Wild with excitement, the children skittered around on the gravel like two young puppies. Happiness like theirs was so precarious, Jane thought, and always running towards extinction. Happiness had to be taken anywhere it could be found. She waited for her husband to lift the children into the car and then she waited for the au pair to sidle into the front seat, rebellion clouding her face.

As the car drove off the two small faces in the rear window shrank into pale fragments. Conversely the garden became huge in the ensuing silence, extended out to the woodland that circled the house like a besieging army.

Jane waited. Am I so afraid of being alone, she wondered, is that it? The trees creaked, their branches enmeshing in a subtle breeze that danced up from nowhere. Its intrusion was deliberate, like the sound that followed it, the rumble of a car coming up the driveway towards her.

SIX

Mrs Quill kept a boarding-house in Shantalla. Originally a council house, it had been bought out in the early sixties by Mr Quill, a small-time builder and well-known GAA supporter (since deceased). The insurance money had given his widow an appetite for business and over the years the house had acquired a number of flat-roofed extensions to accommodate students from the university. Inside, the rooms were cold and cramped and redolent of damp socks.

When Oran knocked on the front door a young man answered. He was massively built with cropped hair and the shoulders of a bull. "Name's Conneally," he said, "Donie Conneally. I'll get Mrs Quill."

As their hands collided Oran winced with pain. "No," he stalled, "just a sec."

Impassively the student listened while Oran hedged around with questions. Suddenly his face broke out in a sly grin. "Tis a love-nest you're looking for," he said.

Oran grimaced at his own transparency. "Is she nosy?" he persisted.

"She's so tight, as long as you pay up she won't

give a curse for your philandering."

Avarice burned inside Mrs Quill like a votive offering. In her eyes every crumb that escaped down her boarders' throats was profit squandered. As Donie had predicted, once Oran paid his rent promptly, ate what he was given and didn't waste electricity by leaving the light on in the bathroom, she took no further interest in him.

University turned out to be a disappointment. It was like school only bigger. Any differences were of scale and a certain architectural idiosyncrasy. The Victorian buildings had the repressed air of a cloister and corridors with splayed gothic windows that didn't let in enough light. At the start of term Oran attended his lectures dutifully. They were sober events held in timbered rooms overlooking the quadrangle or else in a string of prefab buildings scattered through the grounds.

His interest quickly became engaged elsewhere. Galway was full of women and out in Salthill he discovered that the pubs and dancehalls teemed with talent. Methodically he worked his way from one girl to the next until he reckoned he had struck lucky with Marie Fahey. As their bodies bumped together in the crowded dancehall, he learnt that she was a typist who worked in a solicitor's office and that she went dancing three nights a week; that Galway was great crack after Boyle where she came from and that the shops in Galway were lovely only they were terrible expensive. This information jagged through gaps in the pandemonium. By the end of the night her hip-bones were dug into his thighs as they shuffled speechlessly around the floor.

"Would you come home with me after?" he asked lightly as if no other girl had ever refused him.

"After what?"

"After the dance."

"I might."

As easy as that. He couldn't believe his luck.

Marie was a small girl with a neat rounded body of a kind that, over generations, had hauled buckets, milked cows, gathered in turf. She wasn't pretty; her features were too sharp and her hair too grizzled, but she had a pert manner and a way of leaning against him that set Oran's nerves alight. A tiny gold cross glinted on her neck and the fluffy texture of her angora jumper tickled when she sat down on his narrow bed.

Inexpertly he clasped her. She lay back and returned his kiss enthusiastically, opening her mouth and touching his tongue with hers. His fingers traced the tight band of her bra until he faltered on the clasp.

"Don't!" Marie's breath was coming in fat little pants. Oran couldn't keep his hands off her.

"No!" she wriggled out of his grasp. Then she was back, up-close again and blowing in his ear. Her mouth was soft and luscious and her tongue had a life of its own, darting and dancing inside his mouth. His hand dropped into the cleft between her legs. As if in pain she moaned and again, she shot away from him, her face pink with excitement.

"No!" she squealed," nooooo…"

She was like a fish unwilling to be caught and yet unable to let go the line. They wrestled in bed in silence, their writhings more like those of two combatants than of lovers. Then, unexpectedly resolute, she straightened up and pulled her skirt down over her thighs.

"I really have to be going now," she said sweetly.

Outside her digs they stood on the pavement and her eyelashes flickered on his cheek. Without warning, her mouth was on his again, wet and inviting.

"Next time, I promise," she whispered. "Just give me time."

Oran padded his way home across the bridge. The flow of the Corrib had a subdued quality like the murmuring of human voices. At night the city became less alien, its antagonism damped down by the darkness. The character of its routes was becoming more familiar to him; opening up to embrace him at street corners, enclosing him under archways; releasing him at undefined waste places; hugging him close again between walls of carved stone and whitened lintel. He smiled, nurturing the intimacy of her promise, the urgency of her lips on his. "Give me time…" Christ, he wanted so much to get inside a woman that it hurt. Marie was the one, he knew, *Marie was the one*...The phrase jingled in his head as he lay in the darkness of his bedroom and listened to grunts and sighs escaping through the cheap partition walls of Mrs Quill's boarding-house. And like muffled gongs, the uneasy, unfulfilled sounds of adolescent dreams echoed in his imagination.

"A ball-breaker!"

Oran's head jerked up. "What?"

Across the breakfast-table Donie Conneally stretched and then draped his arm over the back of a chair. He stuck a grey, sick-looking tongue at Oran. "Did she give you the old tongue in the ear routine and 'I'm not ready yet, just give me time'?" Oran's spoon slipped out of his grasp and disappeared into his bowl of porridge.

"Stay well away, boy." Pleasantly Donie gazed over Oran's bent head. "Marie Fahey will go to her death a virgin. Better men than you, Gunga Din, have perished on that particular rock-face. She's saving herself, for what, I cannot tell, life being too short. But by the time she gets around to being ready, boy, you'll be too old to know what to do with it." His dark malicious Connemara face smirked.

"I'm doing all right," Oran muttered.

Donie leant across to take the last slice of toast. "A new boy like you needs to be educated in the ways of the world. See our legal system now, have you got the inside track on that?" He looked at Oran and then he opened his mouth wide to shovel in the toast. Oran was bewildered by the direction the conversation had taken. He mistrusted Donie's wide-open expression and his country accent full of soft s's and thick t's that sounded phony as hell.

"I will lay a bet with you," Donie drawled as if he were speaking to a half-wit. "In this town a fellow will end up in court on a charge of assault and he'll get off. Riddle me that now."

Oran shook his head. "Maybe he's innocent?"

"Yerra you must be joking!" Donie was indignant. "I never ran away from a fight in my life."

"Are you in court?"

"I am." replied Donie proudly. "At ten o'clock." He tapped his plate of half-eaten toast and congealed dripping. "This is the breakfast of a condemned man." Oran looked down at the rind of bacon curled up on the plate and wondered, not for the first time, how it was that Donie Conneally got a full breakfast while the rest of the boarders had to make do with porridge. It was rumoured that the bacon and eggs were payment for services rendered, but the notion of Donie threshing about Mrs Quill's bed was too bizarre to be taken seriously. Donie was just one of those people, Oran decided, on whom life bestowed its favours despite, or maybe even because of, their outrageous behaviour. Donie was a chronic student who never passed an exam in his life and spent his days training in the gym. He was renowned for his fighting prowess and any opponent was likely to end up in the casualty department of Galway Regional Hospital.

"A quid I get off."

"What's the odds?" Oran asked.

"The evidence is circumstantially correct, reasonably factual; moreover it happens to be true." Donie eyed Oran. "Are you on? If I'm done you get a quid."

"Make it five shillings."

Donie stood up in disgust. "The man who broke the bank in Monte Carlo."

Oran shrugged.

"Right so, five bob it is." Donie pulled on his jacket. "If I'm not home for my tea you can take it that I'm languishing in Limerick jail and you can tell my white-haired mother that I love her."

Bemused, Oran watched as Donie brushed his hair in front of the mirror. When he had finished, he winked across the glass at Oran.

Like a reproach, a chair stood empty at the tea-table. "Not in?" Mrs Quill shouted as she removed the plate of food before anyone had a chance to eat it. The house buzzed with speculation. Oran said nothing. Donie hadn't been a bad skin but a lunatic all the same and lunatics had a habit of getting themselves locked up. He reckoned his money was safe and that a drink was in order.

In The Galway Hooker Oran pushed through the crowds of students milling around the bar. As he waited to be served, he was jolted by the sound of a familiar accent rising above the clamour of voices. Oran stared. Only a few feet away from him a modern-day Lazarus was holding court, his arms splayed out on the counter.

"It was only mighty!" Donie was wild-eyed with excitement. Then he noticed Oran. "Mine's a pint, new boy," he shouted.

"You got off then," Oran said lamely.

"Without a stain."

Oran could think of nothing to say.

"Out of the very jaws."

Oran edged up the bar, curiosity getting the better of him.

"It was so close," Donie elaborated. "A hair's breadth and from a bad start. Up ahead of me there was a young lad getting hammered and old Calleary on his throne doing the hammering. He was half-way out of a bender and in rare bad form. Half-in or half-way out you couldn't tell, with a head on him like a sliotar after an All-Ireland. Shaking and pouring water into himself like he was leaking through his skin. And the young eejit singing his way into jail. Seventeen years old, first time in trouble, from Bohermore with no job and less chance. Caught robbing a transistor radio and making out he found it. 'Found!' roars Calleary. 'And I'll found you guilty!'

And so he did. Twelve months for robbing a transistor. I'm for it this time, I said to myself. Up the proverbial without a paddle." Donie stopped for a moment as if contemplating an earth-shattering idea. "Lesson one in life, new boy, is that there is nothing," he enunciated slowly, "na-thing to beat a good education."

"Get on with it, Donie," someone pleaded. Donie obliged graciously, taking a swallow from his glass before continuing.

"When I get on the stand Calleary takes a good long look and then he sinks down in his throne like he's going to sleep. No-one says a word. Silence in the court. Then one eye opens. 'The career,' says he 'of this young student is in jeopardy here. Consider the interference to this man's studies…'"

The irony of this was not lost on Donie's listeners and they yelped with laughter. He slammed his glass down on the counter and threw back his head. "The old bastard takes another swig out of the jug. 'Go away and sin no more,' says he and gives me his blessing. 'Case dismissed'."

The pub paused to contemplate the mysteries of the law. Solemnly Donie raised his glass.

"I give you District Justice Calleary," His audience sniggered but Donie's expression didn't alter. "A decent man," he insisted, "and one that would never shite on your carpet." He ferreted around in his jacket-pocket for a cigarette which he took out and lit. Then he sat back on his stool and blew a smoke-ring at the ceiling. "And the Guards," he said seraphically, "were only fit to be tied."

Sprawled along the counter, Donie Conneally epitomised the old axiom about there being no justice in the world. As far as the crowd was concerned, his victory might just as well have been that of innocence over injustice. A blow had been struck generally against authority and in particular, against the Guards. It was an occasion, the pub agreed, worthy of celebration.

Time passed seamlessly. The bar pulsated under Oran's feet and lights swung dreamily about on the ceiling. At one point everyone was bawling that the West was awake. The wave of voices transported Oran as he added tunelessly to the uproar. Until a needle of sound punctured the chorus and the wave weakened and collapsed around him. "Time, lads, please!"

In the street Oran, disoriented by the loss of lights and warmth, lost his way. Buildings loomed up out of the dark and threatened to bury him. Out of nowhere, a voice emerged. "Keep Galway tidy," advised the voice. "Use a litter-bin." Oran clutched at the yellow drum and tried to steady himself. Momentarily he regained his balance and peered around in search of the voice. It was a temporary reprieve. Immediately a sour tide of albuminous sludge tore up his throat. His knees buckled and he found himself kneeling on the ground, the metal drum cool and comforting against his face. Spittle dribbled on to his chin but he was too weak to lift a hand to wipe it away. At that moment, he had only one desire: to die as quickly as possible. Through a vomitous haze he was aware that the voice was addressing him.

"What?"

"I know the very thing," Donie repeated.

Oran groaned. He struggled to his feet. "I'll be all right."

Donie grinned. "A dish of cruibins and chips." Oran retched but Donie was irrepressibly cheerful. He smacked his lips. "It'll put a lining on that old stomach of yours."

Oran buried his head in the litter-bin. The Connemara man sighed and took hold of Oran's arm. Too weak to resist, Oran succumbed and let go of the bin. The two of them stumbled past the closed door of The Galway Hooker.

"Lesson two in life, boy," Donie sympathised wetly into Oran's ear. "It isn't worth a curse, that casual drinking."

SEVEN

O ran sat in the train and watched the city of Galway recede like a complicated dream that, on waking, loses itself in the unconscious. The prospect of being transported so effortlessly out of one world and into another came as a relief after Donie's enticement to ruin and Marie's intransigence on the matter of her virginity.

In Dublin, landmarks greeted him. The grocer's shop on the corner of Pearse Street with sad Christmas lights and faded holly; the Victorian façade of the library. Once familiarity had bred contempt but now distance altered his perspective. There was a homeliness in the tall streets he had never seen before. For years he had done the rounds with his father and had been blind to it. Small details: a note in a letter-box, a broken sill, through a torn curtain a fire burning in a grate. *It's little enough you have to put up with*…On his way home, he decided, he would call on Mrs Gaughan. Already he envisaged her gummy grin that would greet him when he opened her door .

In Fenian Street there was an inexplicable shift in the landscape. The place looked wide open, the way it looked when he stumbled away from Mrs Gaughan and the Legion woman and out into the blessed air of the street. Leaning against the railings, his father had grumbled at him that day for not bringing down a cup of tea. The moment was vivid in his memory. He stopped. The railings were gone but their disappearance did not explain the sense of emptiness. The second-hand shop on the corner was still there and on his other side the pub stood as it had always done.

Then it hit him. The change was so enormous that, like a mouse up close to an elephant, he hadn't been able to see it. As he stood between the shop and the pub he faced into a void. Once a row of buildings had darkened the street. Now there was nothing except a hoarding, flimsy as cardboard and beyond it, an evening sky fissuring above a heap of naked rubble.

At home too, there were changes. Everything in the house looked smaller and shabbier. His father sat rooted in his armchair by the fire like a dead thing that someone had forgotten to clear away. Nellie fussed over Oran with a new, heightened energy.

"There's no-one to talk to now," she complained, "not with the girls married and you gone to college."

Clearly his father didn't count.

"Why don't you go out and enjoy yourselves," Oran urged weakly. She stared at him as if he wasn't talking sense. Her sigh of dissatisfaction set Oran's teeth on edge.

"Where's Mrs Gaughan?" he asked to distract her.

Nellie shook her head. "That poor woman," she said, "never had a day's joy in her life."

"But where is she?"

"The flats got bought up by developers and they stripped the roof with her still inside. The rain got in and next thing, she had pneumonia. All alone and sick, she was. She swore she'd never go to the workhouse but she ended up there all the same."

"Ah, Mam," Oran said irritably, "St James's isn't a workhouse,"

"Maisie Gaughan knew it when it was and she couldn't bear the idea of it, God rest her soul."

Oran stirred his tea slowly. Nellie slapped plates down beside the sink and dried her hands. She held onto the towel, twisting it up into a hard angry knot. When she spoke, her words echoed his thoughts.

"Everything's different," she said and then a new bitterness entered her voice. "Thon gangsters, they have the whole place destroyed."

Oran turned on the television, welcoming the blanket of sound that did away with the need for conversation. Figures scattered in front of burning buildings. Chunks of a street were hurled into the air and arched to land among rows of uniformed men crouched behind high perspex shields.

"Crowd of gurriers," his father complained at the screen.

Then it was the turn of his mother to rise up,

uncharacteristically shrill, and cry, "Billy, you know nothing about it, nothing!"

She crouched down beside the television, her expression a mixture of dread and elation. Oran could tell what was coming next; his father's condemnation; his mother's resistance, their old struggle being fought out on the screen.

"You've never lived with someone's foot on your neck," she said. "Orangemen that would spit as soon as look at you. Battering at the front door on the Twelfth. My God, we took it for so long." And then, in her voice, a note of anguish. "Where will it end? Young wains locked away with their bombs and their bullets. I'm afeard for them all."

Her husband ignored her and glared instead at the television.

"Kalashnikovs," he said loudly.

Impatience stirred inside Oran. "Oh, for God's sake, Da."

"That's what them bandits have hid up their coats."

Their eyes swivelled as a young man came close to the camera. Cloth tied cowboy-fashion over his mouth, he lobbed a stone into the dark phalanx of soldiers. The act of defiance struck a chord inside Oran. The correctness of that stone spinning though the air. He would have preferred to be that boy dancing on the brink rather than be here, in the living-room, listening to his father.

"That's what's behind them," his father said, spittle

whitening in the corner of his mouth. "Communists looking to stir up trouble. I heard one of them on the other night, some little corner-boy shouting about a socialist republic. By God, I'd give it to him. Little pup! Who in this country ever wanted a socialist republic?"

Oran looked evenly at his father. "James Connolly did."

"Don't you dare go twisting history on me, clever dick." His father was shouting, his face purple. "The men of 1916 were true patriots."

"What's the difference? Those people have nothing to lose only their indignity. Now they're fighting back and all you can do is abuse them."

"Indignity!" his father sneered. "Only thing they know is how to hold up a street corner. Give one of them latchicos a job and he'd pass away with the shock. I'd put them in the army. A few years in the army and they'd come out straight."

The row collapsed as quickly as it had begun. His father stabbed at the fire with a poker and then leant forward to switch channels. Hughie Green leered up on the screen, his mouth working overtime as he struggled around the names of a group of Welsh singers. Fresh from the mining valleys and here to entertain us tonight on *Opportunity Knocks*. Billy Reidy sat back in his armchair and let out a quiet belch.

"Or send them off on the boat," he said. "To

England."

His wife stood up and walked out of the room. At moments like these, Oran felt close to his mother. They shared an understanding so deep that they seemed to touch, bone to bone. As the Welsh choir sang, Oran eased himself out of his chair and followed her.

"Where will it all end?" she asked and he thought he had the answer. We shall overcome and power to the people. And one man one vote.

"Yes, but," she said. "Yes, but..."

"Mam, I'm telling you."

Across the kitchen table she looked at him almost lovingly, forgiving him his innocence.

"You don't know," she said flatly, without a hint of doubt in her voice. "You cannot know what it is like, Oran."

But he knew or thought he knew. Wanted to know and to be right. Mammy, listen to me, I'm telling you. The past is dead and we shall overcome.

EIGHT

The train was full of Sunday evening passengers, steaming up the windows and cluttering up the aisles with luggage. As the Dublin suburbs fell away Oran peered out into the darkness and met Galway rushing to meet him in the shape of Marie Fahey. He would tell Marie anything at all that she wanted to hear; that he loved her, adored her. And then he would screw her. He leant back in his seat and yawned. Beside him a young man picked absently at a pimple on his face. He was about the same age as Oran and, like him, he wore denims and thick boots. But the scarf around Oran's neck proclaimed that he was different, that he was a university boy. Idly, he looked over at the newspaper that the man sitting opposite was reading. The man had a beige, civil servant's face and wore a pioneer pin. SPURS BEAT LEEDS...DERBY MOVE UP...P.P. STOPS MASS OVER MINI-SKIRTS. Nothing there to relieve the boredom of the journey. Oran closed his eyes and tried to sleep but the motion of the train jolted him awake. It was an ordinary winter evening. Then the spotty-faced young man left his seat and went up the train to the bar.

When he returned he was transfigured by the news

he brought.

"Were they shot *dead*?" someone asked.

"Yeah!" The young man's eyes bulged. "No-one knows how many though. In Derry, I know that much. They're only getting it on the radio as it comes in. Three or four maybe."

"You're joking!" The middle-aged man sitting opposite was shocked. Then his expression changed. Lowering his glasses he peered at his informant suspiciously, as if the boy's long hair and acne were evidence of some kind of hoax. "Holy Mother!" his voice trailed into silence. Distractedly he ran his hands over his bald head in search of errant strands of hair. "What are they up to at all, at all?"

"Them Brits are murderers," the boy answered him simply.

A fat man with red-brick complexion and hair bushelling out of his ears leant massively across the aisle. "I heard it was more," he shouted as if they were all deaf. "They went on a rampage. Crazy fuckers even killed the little children."

"You're joking!" the middle-aged man said again and rubbed his face in despair.

Some joke, thought Oran.

"So they say," the red-faced man sat back, secure in his knowledge. Oran looked away. The swarm of phantoms was as gradual as a memory unfolding; men and women stumbling and falling, their faces made grotesque by terror. A vision that induced in him, not so much horror, as a sense of responsibility. It settled on his shoulders like a great bird, whose wings flapped open to encompass the exodus of people, their faces straining this way and that, in a pathetic effort to dodge their fate. British imperialism showing its teeth. And not for the first time; in Aden and Cyprus and India and anywhere else that Rule Britannia ever held sway. He knew the score.

From the excited hum of conversation he set himself apart and listened instead to the resonance within. There are impressions too immature for conscious recollection but Oran knew enough to construct a picture. She sat in the old winged chair in the front room, her hair glinting in a stray band of light. Red, was it? No, auburn. Nellie Reidy had been inordinately proud of her auburn hair. And the white blob at her breast was Oran. It was a scene of domestic tranquillity, the sunlight slanting across the dark furniture of carved mahogany and bevelled glass. And one that was shattered in an instant by the sight of Aunt Gertie standing in the doorway, ashen-faced, while outside in the street, a taxi rattled on like an angel of death.

"It's our Shamie..." Aunt Gertie said.

Nellie dragged the baby away from her breast. Vengefully he turned and bawled at a world that dared to invade his contentment. She held him close to her then, so close that he sputtered. Our Shamie, Nellie's favourite brother, for didn't she always tell

Oran that he was the image of his Uncle Seamus?

"What he did for Ireland!" she breathed at Oran, her eyes filling with tears at his sacrifice. "So much..."

Seamus carried messages and forged links. A meeting was set up and he had been given instructions. No-one knew why he failed to meet Martin Twomey, whose photograph adorned the wall of every RUC barracks between Belfast and Maghera. But Shamie never came and five days later, a man's body, swollen and black, was dredged out of the river near Roslea. Accidental death of IRA leader was how the newspapers described it. Local people knew different and they hoarded up the memory of Martin Twomey for future generations, chalking it up as an unpaid debt to the B-Specials.

Uncle Shamie climbed into his bath, only put into the house that Christmas, with shiny new taps and running water and he stained the water crimson with his blood. Death of that kind, at that time, was spoken of in undertones for it was a sin meriting eternal damnation. Unless it was for the Cause. Then it became a martyrdom. But Nellie had no such consolation to carry her through her grief and her sorrow turned inwards to infect the generous flow from her breasts. Oran consumed it all; nourishment for skin and bone and hair and teeth; nourishment too, for the bouts of enmity that surfaced inside him periodically, like the blackened limbs of Martin Twomey emerging from a watery grave.

In the darkness there were bodies everywhere, filling up the ditches, their heads thrown back in a final spasm of agony, their legs spreadeagled in capitulation. Did it matter how many they were? Two or twenty? The bastards, Oran thought, rage beginning to beat in his throat. *Bastards. Bastards. Bastards.*

By now his mother would have heard the news. Dozily bundled up in front of the television. There's never anything on the telly on a Sunday night, she often complained. Well, she had something to watch now. The rattle of guns, the crowd scattering, the awful silence after. Like a flag of defeat a white hankerchief fluttered above a wall and then crabways, a priest scuttled across the line of fire towards the perpetual stillness of a man lying dead in a gutter.

One, two, three, four, five, six.....

No, it can't be, seven, eight, Jesus, nine, ten, Christ, eleven, twelve, O Holy Mother, thirteen.

Thirteen.

Dead.

"It is only a matter of time," his mother had said to him in the kitchen, "before they kill us all."

And he had laughed at her. Out loud.

"Otherwise," she had continued, "why would they be here?"

NINE

In the Church of the Holy Angels, Jane O'Molloy sat down, clasped her hands and let her mind wander. She did not pray. She could not be certain that there was anyone there to hear her. Anyway she was in what is conventionally called a state of sin. She couldn't very well claim a Catholic God and, at the same time, refuse to accept His teachings. Jane had a clear, if simplistic sense of fair play. She was content to sit and indulge her meditative mood.

Despite the lack of prayer she felt she had to come into the church to acknowledge what had happened. Thirteen dead, whoever they were, however misguided, deserved some kind of recognition. She had seen what had happened and would have preferred not to have, but television doesn't allow for such sensibilities. Nothing escaped being dissected by cameras and laid out to be munched over by talking heads. She found it obscene, the sight of those vultures scavenging for newsworthy titbits. Not that she was any different. As much as anyone else she had been rivetted by the images on the screen. What a stupid waste, criminal really, to lead young men astray like that, barbaric to gun them down. One as bad as the other. Involuntarily her head jerked up. A figure lay in a dark street and a priest moved forwards like a swimmer, white handkerchief fluttering from his hand.

Too much! she thought and jumped back on to safer ground.

The interior of the church reminded her of boarding-school; the hypnotic quietude; the constancy of bells and the sanctuary lamp flickering in its red globe; the notes of the angelus quartering out the the day. At boarding-school there was no room for suprise. In winter the daily rosary was recited in the chapel. On summer evenings the girls went outdoors to pray. Hail Mary...Holy Mary...Hail Mary... Holy Mary... Fields slanted away on either side of the gravel path that led to the chalk-white figure on its pedestal. Hands clasped across her breasts, the statue of Our Lady gazed down on the approaching procession. Tower of Ivory...Queen of Heaven... Temple of The Holy Ghost. As she prayed, Jane escaped into another landscape, where fields, stained with red poppies, undulated towards the horizon. Lured by her awakening desire, a daughter went out to lie with a man among the wheat-stalks. And as the stars woke she relinquished herself to him, only to discover her mortality in scarlet splashes across the acres of wheat. Virgin most pure...Mother Immaculate...pray for us, pray for us, pray for us. Hail Holy Queen...

Touching forehead, shoulder, breast, a legion of virgins swore fealty to their Virgin Empress, securing themselves against the ravages of the barbarians massed beyond the convent walls.

Claraville was a school that prided itself in its vocation to educate the daughters of the propertied classes.

"You are privileged girls," Reverend Mother could say without fear of contradiction. "You will become the mothers and wives of the leaders of the country. Yours is a unique vocation; to guide your future husbands and children in the ways of Our Lord and His Holy Mother. This year, we are blessed to receive two girls who have been called to a higher vocation still. *La crème de la crème*. Our two postulants will become, God willing, brides of Christ Himself. In your prayers, please remember your sisters, Mary Pankhurst and Jean Mulhall."

Hanky-Panky and Jinno. Sloughing off their nicknames they disappeared beyond the heavy doors that protected the nuns from the insatiable curiosity of schoolgirls. No girl was permitted down that corridor but they jostled madly for a glimpse. An out-of-bounds raid brought back reports of underwear in laundry baskets. Pink bloomers! Oh delish...

> *Mother Stan was a silly old nun,*
> *Whose knickers were the colour of the sun.*
> *The knicks got mislaid.*
> *How old Stanislaus prayed.*
> *But she still ended up with none on!*

After lights out, smothered laughter persisted in the dormitory until Mother Stanislaus lifted her head from her beads and her angry *girls!* barked down along the cubicles.

Years later, when everyone had forgotten about them, the postulants reappeared in the school chapel. They were dressed in white satin, the folds of material swirling around their ankles as they knelt at the altar-rails, the air thick with incense and the smell of freesias. Throats constricted, mouths sagged as Mother Bridget lifted up a pair of scissors and a silence fell so deep that you could hear the crunch-crunch of the blades as hair landed in whispers on the chapel floor. Why them and not me? Jane wondered, and shuddered as if it were on her own neck that the cold steel rested.

There was a world outside the convent gates, a lesser one, an impermanent world where nothing endured. Fashions rose and sank, wars were fought and brought to an end, heads of state lived and died and were replaced. Within the granite walls there was immutability. Nuns did not age, the tide of uniformed girls was ever in flux. Faces changed but the body replenished itself with impressionable hearts and eyes and puppy-fat legs erupting out of ankle socks.

In the convent grounds the cedars, impervious to season, brushed against a Renaissance sky. On every side, fields nurtured stock and grain to feed the fortified city-state. The suburbs of Dublin were encroaching but Claraville paid no heed to their toy-town streets and spindly lamp-posts. Claraville had the deaths of popes to meditate upon, the intoxicating smell of incense and tallow candles sputtering into flame, the lives of the founders of orders. In winter, low lights chased shadows along the panelled corridors that echoed with the clack of sensible shoes. At Claraville there was Benediction and High Mass and martyrs who went to extraordinary deaths.

And at its core, in the chapel, there was the Omni-Presence, the great listening Ear that heard all and said nothing. It listened to fears and pleas and desires communicated in whispers that, at moments of emotion, penetrated consciousness in a moan that carried across the vaulted air. When the choir began in one sweet harmonious voice the climbing and falling notes of the Gloria, Jane wondered then, if it were not the voice of Christ calling to her, above the heads of her companions, to join Him and become His bride.

Jane stirred in her seat and thought about dinner. Lamb maqlub, she decided, and a decent red. The aubergines seemed firm in the shop. Nothing too elaborate although the camembert looked so gorgeous her mouth salivated at the sight of it. Lemon sorbet ice-cream for afters with cream. A bit wicked, really, since her sister Carol was coming for dinner. Jane was the mother of two children and had managed to hold on to her figure. More or less. Carol on the other hand was fat. There was a lethargy about Carol. Being married to Ken didn't help. He was so retiring that he was hardly there at all. It struck Jane that Carol had married their father or, at least, his type. Vague and ineffectual. Good-looking in a gangly sort of way but with an air of helplessness that engendered in Jane a strong desire to kick him in the shins.

Jane had never forgiven Carol for marrying Ken. Even after all the years and Jane's own marriage and the birth of her children, the memory of Carol's desertion was a hard resistant obstruction in the clockwork.

Jane picked up the skull of a tern from the mantel-piece. In her hand it rolled around comfortingly, so fine that light penetrated the cranium and the delicate jawbones shaped like scimitars.

At home Carol's room had been unlike any other room in the house. Unlike any other room that Jane had ever seen. An aberration of a room. The walls were collages of pictures cut out of magazines, postcards, old newspapers, anything that caught her magpie sister's eye. A patchwork quilt lay on the bed. The iron bed-ends were decorated with brightly painted flowers. Carol made puppets out of papier-mâché and the floor was littered with debris of heads and limbs and black thread. She worshipped Marlon Brando who smouldered at her from a poster above her bed. Along the shelves were ranged books about theatre, film-making, Picasso. Carol's interests were eclectic.

There was something out of control about Carol. It made Mama nervous. Mama liked eveything to be in its place: Dada running his solicitor's firm in Galway, the two girls at school in Dublin. The King in his counting house, the Queen in the parlour, the maid in the garden hanging out the clothes. School holidays were something of an ordeal for Mama, particularly the long summer days when Carol was to be found down in the village in cahoots with the milkman's son. The pair of them would disappear and come in hours late for tea, bearing the half-rotten corpses of small birds and animals which Carol insisted on boiling on the kitchen stove until the skeletons were clean and ready to be strung out across the mantelpiece.

One year an African student stayed in the village. For Carol he was honey to the bee and she loitered with intent around the rectory where he was staying. Mamma had to suffer the sight of his black face grinning at her over the china teacups. At school, Carol expressed startling opinions that she had culled from French novels which she adored because they were printed on brown paper and had their pages uncut. She was found smoking in the garden shed and was threatened with expulsion. Dada had come up to Dublin and talked to Reverend Mother. Jane idolised her older sister but Carol's escapades filled her with dread.

In the centre of the mantelpiece, there was the shell of a sea urchin. Among the fragile skulls its pumpkin shape sat oddly like a fat lady among mannequins.

In the war of nerves, Carol and Jane teamed up against Mama and Dada, particularly against Mama. Jane grew up in a slipstream created by a sister who liked to live along the tidemark of parental consternation.

"Why must she be so difficult!" Mama wailed, crashing her fists down on the dressing-table.

"She'll grow out of it," Dada soothed. "After all, she hasn't done anything dreadful yet."

"Give her time," Mama said darkly. And Mama was right. The pills that Carol stole from the school infirmary were enough to knock her out for days. Even Dada failed to have her taken back by the nuns after her stay in hospital. Jane fretted at school and imagined her sister incarcerated at home, depressed and suicidal. But when she came home for the holidays Jane found Carol entertaining the milkman's son with a stolen bottle of Dada's finest malt whiskey. There had been ghastly scenes according to Carol: Mama shrieking hysterically at her hospital bedside. Jane was unsure whether to believe Carol. In Jane's experience Mama had never done anything as unrestrained as shrieking.

After the summer Carol went away to Dublin to study fashion design and at Hallowe'en she arrived back with Ken, a tall ascetic young man with jutting Adam's apple and pale eyes that protruded when he removed his glasses, which he did frequently in order to wipe them with a grubby handkerchief. Jane surveyed him with astonishment and wondered at the appeal of this pathetic creature for someone who still had Marlon Brando in her bedroom every night.

Beside the sea urchin, a solitary branch of coral, bleached to the perfection of bone.

At Christmas Carol came home and locked herself in her bedroom. Jane was accustomed to her moods and tried not to mind but she missed the conversations that they had, splayed out across Carol's chaotic bed. Morose and lonely, Jane wandered about the house and gradually became aware of an undercurrent in the daily pattern. Scraps of argument escaped through closed doors and reverberated like sounds in a tunnel. Sentences were left unfinished, dangling in the air. All she had were clues to indicate that she was living on the periphery of something beyond her understanding.

When Dada brought her into the drawing-room she followed him, expecting enlightenment. Instead the mystery darkened. Any vision she had concocted was of her own making, an impression of the sides of a box closing up around her sister. Later, in the school library, she found a physical form to put on that vision. An illustration of a mummified corpse, its limbs bound, its face closed in upon its secrets.

"We have something to tell you." Dada gestured her into the drawing-room. Mama was already seated on the sofa. He paused and cleared his throat. "About your sister."

Mama gave an anxious bark.

"Carol is going to marry Ken. We are very happy with the news."

Happy was a funeral bell tolling.

"She'll be getting married next month," Again he paused to clear his throat. "In Dublin."

Jane looked from one parent to the other, at their long twinned faces hinged up like mussel-shells. Between them, the Adam fireplace yawned. Its hearth swept bare was characteristic of the house and the unfulfilled ambitions of its occupants. Dada was sunk in thought. Even when he raised his head and looked across the room to the view beyond the window, she tracked his gaze, partnering him in his quest. But he changed tack and switched his concentration on to the toe of his shoe, stabbing the fender.

"They'll be going away," he announced, "to England."

The air crisped in the room, the temperature

dropping, not just there but everywhere in the house. Coldness permeated every high pale space, laying a coating of frost on the window-panes and freezing stiff the bed-linen in the rooms upstairs. At that moment her sister became a sacrificial corpse, clothed in wedding-white and embalmed in a catafalque. Desperately, Jane rummaged but she could not unscramble the code that her parents were employing. All she knew was the ice-cold barrier pressing against her fingertips. At fourteen years of age she was old and grieving and powerless against the weight of their adulthood.

When she discovered the truth she had raged at Carol for her failure to win out. If only you had confided in me, Jane told Carol in long angry letters that were never sent, the two of us could have run away from home. We could have minded the baby when it was born and there would have been no stupid old Ken to drag along either...

But there was no conviction in her harangue. It was too late. For Jane it was not birth but a kind of death that had taken place between the sheets. And there was further destruction. The collection of bones and shells was swept off the mantelpiece and trampled in an orgy of despoliation that Jane embarked upon, dry-eyed and determined. The maid swept up the shattered pieces and without comment, Mama and Dada carried on, as if the maid had tidied away the whole distasteful business: the baby and Carol and

Ken along with the rest of the debris.

Carol had married Ken in a Dublin church and immediately after the wedding breakfast they had got the boat to Liverpool. When it came to Jane's turn to marry the contrast between the two events could not have been greater. At Carol's wedding there had been ten guests and no publicity. When Jane married Richard O'Molloy, only son of Colonel and Mrs M O'Molloy the wedding was a full-blown society affair with enough money lavished on it to merit a rake of photographs in *Social and Personal* magazine. One hundred and twenty guests came along to witness the ceremony and to drink themselves silly on champagne. At Jane's wedding everyone who was anyone in Galway was there. Even Carol and Ken were there. Sufficient time had elapsed for the sinners to feel free to return to Galway with their three children in tow. At Jane's wedding the cause of their disappearance almost stole the show when Mama and Dada's first grandchild arrived in the doorway of the cathedral. An angel in pink organza, little Caroline scattered rose petals down the aisle for Jane and Dada to walk on. It was an occasion that had all the extravagance of an arranged marriage. And about as much passion.

Jane had remained a virgin, more or less, until Richard. He made such a suitable husband, an up-and-coming architect, talented and intelligent and so very kind. And because, for all these reasons, he was so worthy of her love, it seemed to her that she must be in love with him. Jane had understood that marriage was something one did, preferably with someone one was fond of. And she was very fond of Richard. Sometimes she wondered, however, if she wasn't fonder still of his mother. Their first meeting was lodged in Jane's memory. Birds had sung that morning in the bushes overhanging the ditch where the old woman toiled, her feet encased in wellington boots, her hair tied up in a headscarf, peasant-fashion. She was shovelling out mud with a long-handled shovel that she leant on when she straightened up to greet Jane. There was a gnarled welcome in the old woman's hands and in her words.

"Feel free in my house, daughter," she said simply. This is how people are, Jane had thought, tears pricking treacherously at the back of her eyes.

In the church she heard stealthy movements. A man stepped up on the altar and began to prepare it for mass. A bell rang. Jane stood up. Time to collect the children from school and to drop home Madge's children. The Heaneys were long-standing friends of the O'Molloys. Richard and Garret had gone to school together and, over the years, their families had been linked. Richard had been Garret's election agent; Garret was godfather to the oldest O'Molloy child. They had done well by each other, and had good reason to maintain an association. Politics and the construction industry have a natural affinity. "A relationship of mutual benefit," Richard liked to say, "based on the principle of honour among thieves." Although Jane saw a lot of Madge, she did not think of her as a friend. Their connection, like that of their husbands, was based on contacts. It could be put down to a similarity of class and age and background but the truth, although it was only known to one of them, was that they had only one interest in common; a time-share arrangement on the same man.

No-one knew exactly how Garret Heaney had made his money but, in his fingers, dross turned to gold. A man of opportunity for whom politics was a matter of tactics. When he changed his political allegiance and switched parties it was nothing more than a stratagem to win a seat. In the transition even his speeches didn't need alteration. When he talked of a future there was no perception of progress or, God forbid, of change. Ahead there was either a world run by people like him or else the Dark Age of Anarchy, a pitiless scenario bereft of the paternalism of his caste. Trade, the Great Mover, shifted the world's fortunes about. Commerce, he replied to questions about equity, a rising tide to lift all boats. He could point with some justification to the petite bourgeoisie of Galway that was rising inexorably on the swell created by the multinationals setting up in the new industrial estates in the suburbs of the city.

Garret Heaney was considered one of a new

dynamic breed of politician. At his first outing he had unseated an elderly incumbent who had expected to last out his days in Dáil Éireann. The fact that the ousted man was from Garret's own party had enraged the old guard, but the young members liked Garret's style and his celebration party had ended up with guests jumping into his swimming-pool and fisticuffs on the lawn.

Old Mrs Heaney had worked as a district nurse for thirty years and was known throughout the county. All her life she had idolised Dev. Her son's defection incensed her. The fact that so many people had voted for him because he was Sara Heaney's son only served to fuel the flames of her indignation.

"Turncoat!" she spat at him on one memorable occasion in the foyer of the Great Southern Hotel. "Damn Freestater!"

Her son had refused to take offence. "Mam! There's a powerful spirit in you still," he had laughed, wrapping his arm around her shoulders, "for a woman of your age."

That morning, on her way in to the church, Jane had, by chance, met Mrs Heaney in the street. Although retired from her job, the old woman still wore her nurse's coat, neatly belted and buttoned up to the neck. It gave her a military look and the black ribbon fluttering on her sleeve had all the grandeur of a formal insignia.

"We have seen the Murder of the Innocents!" Mrs

Heaney gripped Jane's arm. "Now we'll be witness to the retribution."

The old woman's eyes gleamed with excitement. She's enjoying all this, Jane thought with revulsion. The event had confirmed everything Mrs Heaney believed in. Jane hadn't the courage to confront the old woman's conviction. Instead she stayed silent, hovering awkwardly on the step until at last, Mrs Heaney lost interest in her and turned to walk briskly away.

TEN

O n the day the thirteen were buried, black flags dragged in the wind in Galway. Clouds moved across the shuttered city to press against the church spires and the sea was lost in a dirty wash that hid any distinction between water and sky. In Eyre Square a group of men leant against an open-backed lorry and waited the way workless men do, without any sense of anticipation. When the change came it was almost imperceptible; a murmur that expanded gradually into a roar as a torrent of people burst out of Shop Street and spread out across Eyre Square.

Oran joined the line of students as they left the gates of the university. The townspeople were more circumspect. Occasionally one stepped forward to join the march but most of them stood silently in their doorways watching the students pass while above their heads, strips of black cloth flapped forlornly. "Come on and join us!" The marchers chanted impatiently but the faces in the doorways barely flickered.

At Nun's Island the march came to a halt. Keyed up by the rhythm of the crowd and the chant of voices, Oran was disappointed by the unexpected stop.

"What's up?" he asked a student beside him.

"It's Heaney's place. The typewriter factory."

Oran strained to see beyond the crowd. In the distance the factory was a jumble of buildings, an extension made from corrugated sheeting tacked on to one side.

"So?"

"The men are on strike and Heaney won't recognize the union."

Oran pushed nearer. A group of men stood outside the gates. Behind them a sign stated that an official trade union dispute was in progress. The men stood stiffly, almost defensively, like mourners at a funeral, holding their caps in their hands.

"Victory to the strikers!" The cry was taken up by the crowd. That did it. As the voices hammered against the factory walls the men raised their heads and smiled triumphantly at the crowd. A young man stepped out of the group. His delicacy gave him the air of a child although a look of determination matured his pale face. Wispy blonde hair, darkened by rain, was slicked down on his forehead. He pulled forward something to show the crowd, a sheet of plywood covered with dozens of typewriter spools that formed a pattern. Intrigued, Oran studied the strange configuration. Then a sudden recognition made his skin prickle.

One and Three. Thirteen.

"Beir bua!" The boy shouted as he lifted up the

placard.

"Beir buaaaaa!" the crowd answered as, slowly the line of marchers began to move off. "Victory to the IRA!"

In Eyre Square excitement flattened into resignation. On the open-backed lorry the microphones didn't work and by the time they were fixed, the crowd was in no mood to be impressed by the first speaker who stood up and spoke in a distorted whine about Liam Mellowes and the demise of the Irish language.

The second speaker startled them by having a Somerset accent. He had mousy hair that flopped down over his glasses. Stuck together with sellotape his spectacles jiggled perilously on his nose as he became impassioned by his own oratory. World Revolution. The Anti-Imperialist Struggle. The Liberation of the International Working-Class. An artistic gent apparently, living in Connemara for the good of his soul. Caught in a frenzy of his own making, the young Englishman spoke until his words ran together so fast that they were incomprehensible. Then the spectacles fell to bits in his hands and half-blind, he stumbled down the steps of the lorry. Around him, the crowd applauded him enthusiastically.

None of the speakers was the man Oran was looking for. He examined the huddle of people on the lorry and was astonished at the sight of the burly frame and shorn head of Donie Conneally. In the name of Jesus, he wondered, what was he at? A drizzle fell as speaker after speaker ploughed through their speeches, intimidated by the microphones and the unreal sound of their voices bouncing off the buildings around the square. The crowd grew restless. A few people began to drift away towards shelter.

When he was called upon to speak, Donie stepped forward to the microphone. For a long moment he gazed pointedly around the square, willing his audience to stay. Then, at last, he spoke. "This is a sad day." he said and fell silent again, shoulders hunched under the burden of his sorrow. The crowd rocked back on its feet, its attention captured. "A sad and terrible day..." He reached out to grip the microphone as if he needed its support. The crowd murmured sympathetically. "These men were our brothers, Irishmen every one, gunned down in their prime." Donie lifted up his arms as if to embrace his audience. It was a gesture of episcopalian dimension. "And what crime did they commit?" His voice sank to a hoarse whisper. Breathlessly, the crowd leant forward. "Only this." He bowed his head, *"They sought justice!"*

Every eye was on Donie. Painfully, deliberately, his head lifted. "They got off their knees and stood like men. And were shot down, murdered like dogs in the street. We have a message for their murderers, a warning for every British soldier that has ever stepped on Irish soil, sword in hand or gun at the ready. We say beware...beware the risen people! And to every killer in uniform that stalks the streets of Derry and Belfast we say *go home*!" Spittle on his cheek, Donie bayed lustily at the wet sky. "Or else, by Christ, we'll send you home in wooden boxes!" The crowd howled. Donie paused again, waiting for silence. When he spoke his voice was almost conversational in tone. "Let us not forget," he continued, "that there are more ways than one to rule Britannia. Starve the bitch or skin the bitch, the result is still the same. I have a message, my friends, which I hope you will take to your hearts. Remember to get Mother England where it hurts. In...her...pocket. I leave you one simple message...*Burn everything British except her coal!*"!

There was a funny popping sound. The crowd murmured as a gun emerged out of the sea of faces and pointed to the sky. Pafff! The noise it made was comical, like a child's toy, but it was the real thing all right. A student nudged Oran. "See him?" he said. "That's Brian Walsh." A glimpse of heavy jowl and black beret, a flash of khaki. It was enough. Oran plunged into the crowd on the trail of his quarry.

He found the two men standing close to the lorry. They looked out of place in the youthful crowd. More than just age set them apart, an air of seriousness, maybe even of dejection, it was hard to tell, hung around them. Brian Walsh was the bigger of the two. He stood awkwardly, the way big men sometimes do, round-shouldered, hands lost in the pockets of an army surplus coat. An overweight, shambling, untidy-looking man. His movements were ponderous and clumsy as if he moved through deep water. A thoughtful look settled in his face as he sucked on an unlit pipe. Oran got the impression that under the combat jacket and black polo-neck jumper there was skin as soft and unblemished as a baby's.

In contrast, his companion was slight as a whippet, older, with thinning hair and an expression of watchfulness in his eyes that darted this way and that as he spoke. Dominick Keegan had a mongrel look, underfed and suspicious, and the air of a man who lived on his nerves. A narrow smile illuminated his face as he spoke and then faded as quickly as it appeared. Oran cleared his throat. "Young men are needed for the struggle," he said. Startled the two men looked at him. "And I want to join up." Even to himself the words sounded false. For how long had he wanted to express his sincerity, to explain the understanding he had arrived at, through the long hours lying awake in the dark? And now that he had his chance, his words sounded lame and unconvincing.

What have we here? His listeners' suspicion was palpable. Their eyes collided with one another, exchanging hidden messages.

"Is that a fact?" Dominick said almost jokily. Oran nodded. The look in the man's eyes was sharp. Wary.

Another lull and then Brian said something in his soft burr.

"What?"

Brian Walsh extracted the wet end of his pipe from his lip. "You're a student?" he repeated. Shtoodint. The way Donie Conneally said it.

"Yes."

"Well," said Brian gravely, "you must have a great education then." Oran raised his eyebrows and tried to look disparagingly at his great education. This was no conversation to be having with such men. He turned to look at Brian Walsh but the older man's expression was a mystery; an unfocused stare that wavered across Oran's face and then shifted off in to the distance.

"Not from Galway?"

"No."

Brian pulled down his lip and sighed.

"From Dublin," Oran said.

While the two men digested this information none of them said anything. Eyre Square was emptying fast. Oran sould see a line of students straggling down towards the docks where, he learnt later, they took over the offices of an insurance company with a head office based in Leeds. Theirs was a polite occupation. The office-girls welcomed the unexpected diversion and for their part, the students wandered around the offices, unfurling a banner before withdrawing, honour satisfied, to the nearest pub.

"Okay." Dominick twitched his head around. "You can come down on Tuesday to the meeting. Politics only, mind. Sinn Féin." Oran nodded, grateful for anything.

Time, he told himself, would prove to them the extent of his commitment. He had made the first move and that was the main thing. In Shop Street the rain had stopped and a pale light struggled through the banks of cloud and glinted off the shop-windows. Galway had never looked so appealing.

Outside a newsagents, Donie Conneally was leaning up against a lamp-post. Oran opened his mouth to tell him his news and then quickly slammed it shut again. Jesus! What could he have been thinking of! He nodded at Donie.

"That was some speech," he said.

"Aye."

"Really good."

"Well," Donie said modestly, "someone had to say it."

"But you did it so well."

"Burn everything, eh? It's a good line." Donie was lost in admiration. "Gets them right in the solar plexus." Oran nodded. It had been a good speech and one that needed saying. He had to admit that he had misjudged Donie.

"The bastards," said Oran.

"Oh, the cunts," agreed Donie amiably. He stepped

aside to let Oran walk past him. As he did so Oran glanced down at the copies of the *Daily Mirror* and the *Guardian* that Donie was carrying.

"These, boy? Yerra," Donie said as he waved the newspapers under Oran's nose, "they're only for burning on the fire." And then he winked. A big comfortable wink of someone who was enjoying a piece of comic entertainment.

"You..." Oran's mind went blank. The gulf was immeasurable between the two men he had just parted company with and the one standing in front of him. For a moment his mind was blank. This was important. Serious business. At last he found the word he was looking for and he leant forward, enjoying its satisfying resonance. "*You dilettante!*" Oran hissed. But to his annoyance, Donie whooped with laughter.

ELEVEN

O nce you become a subversive you are never alone. From that moment on, a surveillance apparatus billows in your wake. No matter what you do or where you go, you carry an impression of men watching. You make allowances for the telephoto lens, the hidden tape-recorder, the telephone tap.

Just in case.

Sometimes you suspect that they have tunnelled an entry into your brain and are on the inside, taking down everything in triplicate.

TWELVE

The shed was deserted. He couldn't believe it. He had been conned. They hadn't trusted him after all. He sat down on a bench overlooking the river and stared at the swans idling on the water.

Just when he was about to leave, Oran saw a familiar figure in the distance. Dominick Keegan was whistling as he cycled along the footpath towards him. As the older man drew near, he dismounted carefully and pulled a key out of his pocket.

"Handy place to meet," he addressed Oran cheerfully. "No-one ever thinks of looking here."

Inside, the shed was empty apart from piles of ladders stacked up against a wall and a clutch of sweeping brushes resting against a tower of office chairs. Dominick began to dismantle the tower as he placed three chairs side by side in the middle of the floor and then set another three chairs facing them. They both heard the car pulling up outside. Dominick cocked his head. "That's them."

Massive in his army coat, Brian Walsh lurched into the room accompanied by an elderly man.

"Luke Feighery."

There was a countryman's welcome in the way

the old man took Oran's hand in his. The man's features were surprisingly patrician. Tufts of hair sprang out above his finely-pointed ears giving him a look of startled innocence and his cheekbones swelled like pebbles beneath papery skin. Luke Feighery lived with his father, a small farmer, on a holding outside the city. It was difficult for Oran to envisage the living parent of anyone as old as Luke. "But the Da's a healthy old dog," Luke snickered. And capable still, it was obvious, of exerting authority over his only son.

Brian and Luke were followed into the room by two young men. One of them was only a schoolboy, tall and skinny and drooping like a forced daffodil. Overcome with embarrassment, he rolled away from Oran and, avoiding the chairs lined up expectantly in the middle of the room, he collapsed on the pile of ladders.

"Kwee-veen." Airily Dominick waved an introduction at him but Oran's attention was fixed on the young man who had followed the schoolboy into the room. The blonde fringe and frail features were unmistakable. It was the young man who had raised the placard outside Heaney's factory. He glanced at Oran and then swung a chair around and straddled it. Burying his chin in his folded arms the young man gazed at the floor.

The meeting dashed Oran's expectations. There were long wrangles about money. Luke Feighery was treasurer and patently unfit for the office. When asked about finance, his hands fluttered upwards in agitation. Bills from the Árd Oifig were read out, for newspapers sold and not paid for, for subscriptions to funds for prisoners' dependents. As the litany lengthened, the old man's hands became like two white birds struggling desperately to break free. "I cannot understand it at all." he said helplessly.

No-one said anything. Then Brian picked up another letter.

"A chairde," he read. "Our aim is to strengthen the people's resistance against the forces of oppression. The people of the Six Counties are rising up to shake off the twin tyrannies of Orange bigotry and British imperialism. Forces are rallying in order the smash this resistance of Catholic people to their oppressors. Our role is to be in the vanguard leading the way forward towards a new Ireland. One that will be Gaelic, independent and free." Brian reached the end of the letter, in which all members were exhorted to increase sales of the newspaper and to make sure that Easter commemorations were held in all areas thoughout the country, to honour the Republican martyrs who had fought and died for the cause of Ireland and to ensure that the Stickies didn't get a foothold on traditional commemorations to which they had lost all claim and title, being nothing more than cowardly lackeys of British interests in Ireland....

The bills were forgotten and Luke's hands rested

contentedly on his lap. The smoke from Brian's pipe drifted up in a ruminative spiral.

"The commemoration will be held as usual," Dominick said. "I will contact Lar Morrison about the arrangements. You'll have the pipes, Luke?" Luke Feighery nodded happily. "We'll have more about the commemoration after," Dominick continued, "Any other business?"

Silence.

Then, "Yes."

Everyone turned to look at the young man with the blonde hair.

"I want to ask a question."

It was the first time he had spoken since the meeting began. In a flat city accent he directed his statement at the three men facing him.

"Away you go, Fergus," Dominick, the chairman, gave way.

The boy chewed on his lip. He hesitated, his glance swept around the walls of the shed before he spoke. "This letter there is about the resistance of the people. Well, I want to know what you're going to do about the resistance right here in Galway."

The three men looked at him in silence. Slowly Brian pulled his pipe out of his mouth and tapped the bowl against the leg of his chair. Tock tock tock. The noise sounded hollowly in the silence. "What's that?" he asked in his muffled voice.

"You know very well." Fergus's reply was swift.

Angry. At the sound of dissension Kevin, the schoolboy, stirred out of his torpor. He sat up, quivering with anticipation as Fergus focused his belligerence upon the ceiling. "You'd think nothing ever happened in this country only in the Six Counties," he complained. Dominick hissed gently but the young man ignored him and turned instead to Oran. "Amn't I out on strike at this very moment and fighting for my rights?" he asked. Bewildered by the unexpected turn of events, Oran looked to Dominick for guidance but the older man pursed his mouth and said nothing.

"I left school at fourteen and I've been working for five years for Garret Heaney," Fergus continued, "And that man is suppposed to be a TD. Over in the factory there's no canteen nor nothing. Only a bog out the back and twenty of us assembling typewriters in a dump and getting only shillings for our trouble." Fergus paused. A smile flitted across his face, a hard grimace that died in an instant. "Oh, a right Irishman is Garret Heaney. I meet him every Sunday at mass in the Claddagh and he wouldn't give you the time of day."

"Ah now, now," Dominick said soothingly. "What can we do about it? Garret Heaney is a hard case all right. A Freestater and a turncoat. Even his own mother never forgave him for changing over."

"What can you do?" In answer the young man's gaze swooped down from the rafters and fixed on to

Dominick's face. "Christ!" He folded his arms across his narrow chest and blew out his cheeks in a welter of disgust. "A bomb wouldn't be out of the question."

Kevin, the schoolboy, gave a girlish giggle and smothered it fast with his hands. Dominick scowled at Fergus. He was about to speak when Brian's voice struggled up through clandestine mists.

"Our job is to support the struggle in the Six Counties," Brian said fiercely. "Nothing can jeopardise the Cause. The Republican movement is fighting for the day when the four parts of Ireland will be free. Then we can build a new Republic."

"That's it," Dominick concurred. "That's the very thing." Beside him, like a mechanical toy, Luke Feighery nodded his head and patted the air with his hands. A united front. Defeated, Fergus slipped further in to his chair. No-one spoke.

Then Fergus lifted his head and wiped his fringe out of his eyes. "And in the meantime," he said, "Garret Heaney can screw us into the ground."

It was a bitter postscript. Along the wall Kevin, the schoolboy, sank back onto his nest of ladders and closed his eyes.

"Men like him have their uses," Dominick said mysteriously. Brian straightened up and noisily shuffled the letters in his hands.

"Well, well," Dominick's gaze wandered around the room in search of inspiration. "So that is the way of it." No-one stirred. "I therefore declare the meeting over." Still no-one stirred. The three men looked at Oran and bemused, he returned their quizzical looks. He got the message and stood up.

"You'll be with us on Easter morning." Dominick said cordially. Oran nodded and walked across the room to the door, his footsteps thudding like gunfire on the concrete.

Evening had drawn in and the city was lit up. Along the margin of the footpath the river lapped quietly. Unable to make up his mind to leave, Oran dawdled along the bank of the river until, suddenly resolute, he turned back on his tracks. When he arrived outside the shed again he skirted the wall of the building until he found an empty oil-drum standing below a high-level window. His curiosity was insatiable. By climbing up on to the drum he was just about able to peer in through the window and view the scene he had just left.

Inside, the chairs had been moved back against the wall and a large space created in the middle of the room. Dominick was standing, military-style, hands behind his back, at ease. Facing him, the others were lined up in formation. Each man wore a black beret and in his hand, held a long-handled sweeping brush as a surrogate gun.

Sweeping brushes! An uncontrollable desire to laugh swept over Oran. Just then the schoolboy Kevin dropped his sweeping brush with a loud clatter and he fell to his knees, his face purple with embarrassment, and grabbed hold of the handle. Unnerved by the sound, Oran jumped down from the oil-drum and crept away.

He was almost at Mrs Quill's gate when a car slid out of nowhere and drew up beside him. A door swung open. "Get in."

"Like fuck I will!" Oran was cocky. Who were these guys? He'd never seen them before. Two big guys in open shirts and shiny suits.

"Special Branch, Reidy." The man's face was chubby and framed with brown teddy-bear curls. Oran's mouth dried to dust. He said nothing and climbed into the back seat.

"That's better." The fat one grinned and moved along the seat to give Oran space. Soon they were out of Galway and along the Headford Road. Flat glistening fields heaved away from the window. In the gathering dusk, Lough Corrib shone dully in the distance like pewter. Bleak country with not a tree for shelter and the sight chilled Oran to the bone. Anything could happen to him out here.

"Not much movement on the lake so far," the driver said conversationally.

The fat man stirred. "Early days. Caught a few off Knockferry last week but it's poor enough. Too many chasing too few." His mournful, red-rimmed eyes settled on Oran. "Fisherman, by any chance?"

Oran shook his head.

"Pity." The fat man redirected his attention towards

the distant lake. *Pitypitypitypitypitypity*. The word vibrated in the air, a tremulous, abandoned sound.

At Annaghdown the car turned off the main road and inched down to the lakeshore before coming to a halt. In the silence Oran could hear the sound of water lisping over the stones. Inside, the air was muggy with cigarette-smoke and the scent of a cardboard air-freshener dangling from the rear mirror.

"Now why would a young lad like you be mixing with scum?" The fat man draped his arm along the seat and wriggled closer to Oran. "Wouldn't you be better off now, sticking to your studies?" Oran said nothing. Cautiously he stretched out his cramped legs and waited. The man's face opened in a wide-gapped grin. "Or maybe studying how to stick it into Marie Fahey."

Oran swore at him, Instantly the man grasped Oran's collar and yanked his head forward to land him hard down into the suffocating folds of his coat. Gagging, Oran was, with the shock of it. Tears burnt his eyes. Oh, mother, where are you now? Above him the fat man was yelling and he had the ice-cold circle of his revolver stuck into Oran's temple and Oran knew for sure that the bastard could squeeze that trigger. Wheeeeee! Just for the sheer hell of it and no-one would ever know. For sure!

But the fat man grunted suddenly and burrowed away into the corner of the car. Oran rose up, hammering at the door with his fists, spluttering and roaring. In the front seat the driver wound down the window and threw out a cigarette-butt while his companion in a leisurely way returned his revolver into its holster.

"Don't you know who I am?" he asked softly, "I'm Matt Moran."

That struck home. Oran stopped his futile racket. Mad Moran. Dominick had warned him about Mad Moran who took a special interest in subversion.

"Nice country around here. Beautiful lake." Moran continued, "You could lose a man in it and no-one would ever know."

Involuntarily Oran stared out at the dark ripples of water. He didn't flinch when Moran tapped his cheek, the way a lover might, and said, "We can take you any time. Don't give us cause, Reidy."

In Shantalla, when the car stopped, Oran grabbed at the door. It opened immediately. But just as he reached the pavement, the Special Branch man leant out and hooked his plump knuckles on to Oran's wrist. "I know that scum call me Mad Moran," the man said. "What they say about me is true." Lazily he smiled his woolly smile at Oran. "Every word. In my job it pays to be crazy. It takes one to know one…"

Across the road Donie Conneally was sauntering in the direction of Mrs Quill's front gate. Encouraged by the sight, Oran wrenched his arm free of Moran's grasp and made a run for it. "Hey Donie!" he yelled, never so glad to see anyone before. Donie Conneally

slowed down and stared at him. Then he saw the
Cortina swing around on the road and disappear out
of the housing estate.

"Funny company you keep," he said and looked
curiously at Oran.

Oran shrugged his shoulders and said nothing.

"Are you all right?" Donie was solicitious. Oran
didn't answer. His vision clouded and he was afraid
that he might pass out. He felt rather than saw Donie
beside him, as he linked his arm in Oran's. Casually,
as if the two of them had been out for a stroll, they
walked towards the house and the best he could
manage was a wild, quavering, strangled "*fucking
scum...*"

"I'll drink to that," Donie said stoutly. His laughter
wrapped itself over Oran like a thick cloak. "But then,
as you know, I'll drink to anything."

Afterwards, seated at the table in Mrs Quill's dining-
room, Oran tried to rid himself of the taste of his fear
with platefuls of fried bread and gravy. As he
swallowed the food, he prayed to God that Matt
Moran knew nothing about the sweeping brushes.

THIRTEEN

"**G**alway is a West Brit town," Dominick said. This news came as a surprise to Oran. Dominick explained. "A useless place when it came to fighting the British. That's why we have to go outside for the commemoration."

Knuckles whitening on the steering-wheel, Brian Walsh drove them through the landscape of his myopia. How much his world resembled the real world was anyone's guess, for he refused to acknowledge any weakness in his eyesight. More than anything, Brian was fascinated by strength. Particularly military strength. Power comes out of the barrel of a gun, he was fond of quoting, his gaze creeping across the illustrations of firearms that decorated the walls of the house where he lived with his mother. On the chimney breast he had painted the crude outline of a man in battledress, sprouting a tricolour.

"Time to collect Luke." Ever vigilant, Dominick sat on the edge of the front passenger seat. When the car pulled up outside a bungalow, he got out and returned with Luke Feighery, who was carrying a long case. Close up, in daylight, Luke's face was red and scored with skin ulcers. His fingers drummed silent tunes on the back of the seat and then dropped down shakily between his thighs. Kevin, the schoolboy, sat on Oran's other side and chewed fiercely on his fingernails. As the car advanced past the stone-walled fields of East Galway the only sound to break the silence was the wheeze emanating from Luke's bronchitic chest.

Their destination was a town with a wide main street and a memorial to the men of 1916 squatting among sweet-wrappings and broken bottles. The street ribboned up beyond the church where railings, freshly painted a Virgin Mary blue, enclosed rows of parked cars. Buildings gaped in an empty morning light. Mass was in progress and, as if by implosion, the life of the town had been sucked in behind the doors of the church.

"Keep your eye on that door," Dominick instructed Oran. "When they start to come out, give us a shout." Feeling conspicuous, Oran leant against the railings as the others melted in among the cars. A silence fell, broken only by the sound of sporadic muffled barks. Oran tried to concentrate but his attention was distracted by the sounds punctuating the quiet morning. Curiosity triumphed and he edged his way between the cars until at last, peering along the gap between the wheels of a parked lorry, he found what he was looking for.

Four pairs of boots jabbered on the tarmac. A disembodied voice rose into a shriek of exasperation.

"*Clé, deis, clé, deis...*" It was Dominick. "Jesus Christ! What are you doing? *Clé...Clé...Clé*, I said!" Blithely the eight army boots continued their mad uncoordinated battering on the ground. Afraid his laughter would be heard, Oran ran back to his post only to discover that, in his absence, the doors had opened and there were people standing on the church steps.

"Dominick!" he yelped. At first there was no response. Then Luke Feighery emerged from behind the lorry. Gripping his pipes against his dirty tartan kilt and frowning horribly, he forced through a few garbled notes. Not of music, more like the beginnings of music, unformed and tuneless. Dominick followed him, carrying a tricolour. Bringing up the rear, and still lamentably out of step, marched Brian and Kevin.

Each face bore an identical expression; solemn, reverential, their eyes fixed on some distant point. Oran felt a tugging inside him. At that moment, the men coming towards him formed part of a thread linked back into history, unbroken for as long as men carried the tricolour on Easter morning. In a haze of sentiment they drifted past him and down the street towards the memorial where the little contingent came to a halt. The sound of the pipes drained away. The day shimmered emptily. At their backs the church doors swung closed. Even the few communion-shirkers who had slipped out early before mass was over, had disappeared. A lone newspaper-seller remained on the steps of the church.

Oran ran down the street. "You'll have to do it again," he shouted.

Luke Feighery was the first to break ranks. His face swung around, puce-coloured and clammy with sweat. "Can't...no puff left...you..." contempt spewed out between the rasping gulps of air, "shtoodint!"

Oran was the only one to feel bad about his mistake. The others were surprisingly philosophical about it. They were accustomed to failure and even, he discovered, took a peculiar solace in it. The unstated concensus was that if the town had missed the commemoration, then it was the town's loss. A duty done, regardless of circumstances, was a duty to be celebrated. Carefully Luke arranged his war pipes into their case while the others rolled up the flag before making their way down the street towards the Ranchero public house.

Just then the church doors opened. Streams of people poured out of the porch and moved down the steps and on to an arid desert where only minutes before, there had briefly bloomed the flower of Irish manhood.

"I thought Lar Morrison would be there, mind you," Brian said on the way back to Galway. "I gave him good notice."

"You'd think with the commemoration being in his home town."

"Old comrades, eh?"

"You would expect it of him."

"He should have been there all right. When he wasn't in the Ranchero I thought maybe he was away somewhere."

"Away in Ballinasloe, you mean!" Kevin the schoolboy chipped in.

Luke let out a snicker of laughter. Oran raised his eyebrows at Kevin. In reply the boy twirled a finger on his temple.

"Give over that talk," Brian said vehemently, "There was never anything wrong with Lar Morrison only his nerves gave him a bit of trouble one time. You'd think it was a crime."

"To be sure," Dominick said sagely.

Kevin rolled his eyes and said nothing.

"And Fergus never turned up either," Brian said.

"He told me he didn't think there was any point." Kevin rubbed his chin with his hand, enthusiastic in his tale-telling. "He said he'd rather be on picket duty."

Dominick cleared his throat and opened the window to empty his phlegm into the night air. It was a moment of sobriety in the talking and singing and good humour that transported them back to Galway. Brian peered into the dark ahead and muttered.

"Never any good," Dominick agreed. "Fergus was never any good. A terrible man for asking questions. And what for?" He appealed to the others, "We all know what we stand for, isn't that right?"

Their assent came rumbling up to satisfy him.

"His father was in the Freestate army," Luke piped up. "You could never trust a man like that."

A spy, maybe. The thought settled over them. An awkward intrusion of an idea. Christ, Oran thought, I hope they don't think I'm a spy.

As if reading his mind Dominick turned to face him. "What about you?" he asked.

Oran's head shot up. "What?"

"Did you say you were looking for work?"

"I will be," Oran said, relieved. "There's only four weeks left before term ends and then I'll have to get work somewhere. If there's nothing around Galway I'll go away to England on the buildings."

Brian spoke. His words hummed like a bluebottle in a jar. "There's work here, if you want it."

Dominick said, "Oh?"

"Out towards Bearna. O'Molloy's place. He's one of them architects. Bought a mansion out that way. I've just finished up a job for him. He's looking for a labourer and they have money, mountains of it, the kind that buys chandeliers for all the bathrooms." Brian shifted around in his seat. Fleetingly his gaze slid across Oran's face.

"Tell him I sent you," Dominick said cheerfully but the words didn't match the impression that Oran was left with. He had a feeling that he was being put on trial. Unsure of the reason for their sudden interest, he hesitated and then wordlessly, nodded into the dark.

The journey ended in Dominick's kitchen. He lived in a council estate on the backside of a hill bordering the city. The house was full of children who watched each slice of bread and margarine that Dominick's wife offered the visitors. Their breakfast, thought Oran, and the bread turned to cotton wool in his mouth.

"Hold on there a minute," Dominick said and left the room. In his absence the men were smitten with shyness. Dominick's wife stood by the uncurtained window, eager to please and yet unable to find an opportunity. The kitchen was skeletally furnished: a few chairs, a table, a cooker, a television on an upturned crate and a cupboard. Nothing else except a plaque with Home Sweet Home inscribed on it and a torn copy of the Proclamation stuck up on the door. The walls were stained with mould and flaking plaster and reeked, unmistakably, of poverty.

"Howzat!" A fancy-dress figure leapt into the room. Dominick had wrapped a saffron-coloured kilt around his waist and pinned it together with a nappy-pin. Above the animated faces of the children his wife's mouth broke open in a paroxysm of delight, exposing a jumble of rotten teeth. Encouraged, Dominick began to dance a jig on the kitchen floor and the room was infused by a sudden incongruous gaiety. As he lit his pipe Brian allowed himself a smile. Draped against the table, Kevin shuddered with embarrassment.

Beside him, Luke Feighery was convulsed in a rush of high-pitched laughter.

Inexpertly Dominick flung his body around. There was a boyish abandon about the way he stamped on the floor, his arms twitching along his sides, his face contorted with concentration. Then his performance came to an abrupt end and the tumult of laughter disintegrated into a babble of conversation. Satisfied, he jumped up on the table and sat perched on the edge, a slice of bread in one hand and a cup of tea in the other.

Later in front of the faded text of the Proclamation he raised a hand for silence.

"In the name of God and of the dead generations from which she receives her old tradition of nationhood, Ireland through us, summons her children to her flag and strikes for her freedom. Having organised and trained her manhood through her secret revolutionary organisation, the Irish Republican Brotherhood..."

On his hips the kilt looked ridiculous, askew and trailing down his calves, but Dominick was oblivious of anything except the words issuing from his mouth like an incantation. And in that swaying, drunken group Oran felt again the tug, tug, tugging. The old statement of intent. Sheltering together against the dark forbidding fields that rolled to the horizons of night, he was not alone. As they stood there, in that shabby kitchen, they were united by the words and by the dreams beyond the words.

Dominick's wife had planned her ambush carefully. It took place when they were getting ready to leave. Unnoticed in the crush of men moving out through the narrow hall, she placed her hand on his sleeve. Her back was angled to block out any possibility of Dominick witnessing her petition. "Will you give us a lend..." The request escaped from her mouth like a sigh and the look in her eyes, cold with anxiety, wiped the grin off Oran's face. Being broke, he could refuse her easily, without a qualm. She held on, no longer touching him physically, but the intensity of her need still demanding a response.

Oran remembered the money lying in his bank account. On the last occasion he had been home his mother had stuffed a five-pound note into his hand, a secret gift, without his father noticing. Now it seemed as if his mother needed that money back. The way the woman stood before him sparked a memory and that child, hiding at her skirt, could have been him once. Their wordless insistence undermined him and before he could prevent it, she had him implicated in her conspiracy.

"Tomorrow then," he muttered, "outside the bank."

And without another word, she turned her back on him, as if they had never spoken.

FOURTEEN

"Y is?"

"Is Mrs O'Molloy in?" Oran asked. Blankly, the au pair looked at him. On her upper lip there was a line of black hair that matched the pubic-like hair bunched around her ears. Oran tried again.

"Dominick Keegan sent me out." Sunlight streaked down the hall, illuminating ornate picture-frames, a crystal chandelier, heavy embossed wallpaper. Here was money and lots of it.

"Who is it, Monique?" A new voice this time. Languid, upper-class cool. The au-pair stepped back to give way to a woman standing at the end of the hall. The woman had an untidy head of hair wrapped up in a scarf and a pair of intelligent grey eyes. Old paint-stained shirt, jeans, bare feet. Oran had placed someone else in the setting; someone older and finer, not this freckled young woman in dirty clothes. Involuntarily he looked down. The sight of her feet on the rich carpet threw him off-course, with their knobbly toes askew and thick with dust.

"Come in, come into the kitchen," she cried. "Will you have a cup of tea?"

Her warmth drove him further into confusion. He

was prepared for the lady of the manor treatment, negotiations at the tradesman's entrance. He hadn't expected to be invited in like a guest. Unwillingly he followed her into the kitchen. It was a big comfortable room with cream-coloured cupboards lining the walls and an Aga stove shining at its heart.

"Well?" she asked lightly.

"Dominick Keegan said you had work."

"How is the old villain?" There was barely a trace of West of Ireland in her voice. "I told him three sockets in all the rooms but I might as well have been talking to myself." She picked up the kettle. Oran stood in the middle of the floor and said nothing. "For heaven's sake, sit down. Have a ciggie and relax," she ordered, pulling up a chair. "What do you think of the house? It's magnificent isn't it?" She didn't wait for a reply, but waved around her. "You wouldn't believe the condition of this place when we moved in. Damp, wet rot, dry rot. We spent the first six months ripping eveything out and the second six months putting it all back together again." Oran extracted a cigarette from the pack. Benson and Hedges Gold. He was tempted to take two. None of your Sweet Afton crap here. He lit up and then looked around at the gleaming ceramic and mahogany.

"It's well for some." What the hell did he say that for? Did he want the job or not?

"Jesus," she drawled. For a moment her eyes flickered with astonishment. He could sense her amusement as if he had said something funny instead of offensive. "You're right, of course," she was smiling openly at him now, "but you have to understand that we are the deserving rich. In Ireland that's the only kind there is. If you walk into a pub and you're down and out, nobody wants to know. If you're doing well someone will always buy you a drink. What's known as greasing the bum of an overfed pig."

It was Oran's turn to be startled. She laughed, a plummy laugh that had him grinning despite himself. "That's better." Satisfied, she placed a mug of tea in front of him and then sat down. "Anyway," she continued, "at the rate we're spending money on this house we'll soon be the undeserving poor." She proffered a grimy hand. "Me Jane. Who are you?"

"Oran Reidy."

"And you're looking for work?"

"Yes, I'm working my way through college."

Her eyebrows lifted. "Well," she said, "I don't think we can pay you enough to see you through college but if you want it, the job's yours."

"You don't know anything about me," Oran protested.

"Oh yes, I do. Dominick told me all about you. With your experience you should do fine."

Christ, what yarn had Dominick spun the woman?

"Do you want to see it?"

"What?"

"The studio, of course." She stood up quickly, and

opened the kitchen door. Outside there was a large cobbled courtyard. On three sides there were outbuildings and the house itself made up the fourth. The buildings were constructed of red brick, mellow in the sunlight. Most of them were in ruins with sagging roofs and weeds sprouting from crevices. The floor was an uneven patchwork of puddles of water and cobbles and clumps of grass. The courtyard had an abandoned look, and yet the windows of the outbuildings gave off a vigilant air as if they harboured life. If they did, it was an occupation by marginal creatures; mice and bats, owls and ghosts. Over years of neglect the buildings had reverted back to the wild, and their openness had made them accessible to a population that lived by its wits.

Jane led Oran towards a two-storey building which still had a roof and windows. As the key grated in the lock there was a half-caught response, the sound of tiny feet scurrying across the floor, hidden disruptions in the straw. Inside the air was cool and dark and smelt of cidery apples. Jane crossed the floor and mounted the narrow stair leading to the first floor. As he followed her, Oran was conscious of the nearness of her legs branching above his head.

When they stepped into the attic room the atmosphere was pungent with the scent of unseasoned wood. A wonderful smell, redolent of pine and moss and bramble. In the future, that infusion of woodland would evoke in Oran a sense of sanctuary, of last refuge. But for the moment, innocent of meaning, the smell hung lightly in the room. It was a large loft with two dormer windows set into the steep roof. At one end, a door stood ajar and Oran caught a glimpse of a bath and wash-hand basin hanging off its brackets. Planks of timber were stacked in neat piles along the white-washed wall.

"Don't you think it's perfect?" breathed Jane. He glanced at her. Her face was stripped of its know-ingness. She looked unsure of herself. Vulnerable. Tendrils of hair floated onto her blue shirt-collar. There were fine lines demarcating the planes of her face, along each side of her mouth and under her eyes. Her determined jaw gave way to a delicate slightly crêpy neck. What age was she? Were it not for the telltale lines mapping her skin, she could have been a child, with that look of uncertainty and the streaks of dirt across her face. "I've been doing a bit of work on the place. I knocked down all the partitions but the floor needs replacing. There's other work too, of course, but I'm in no hurry. What do you think?" she asked.

Oran shrugged. She was the boss. It was work.

"The Corboys owned this house for generations. The house itself is made of stone but for some reason they imported the bricks from the North later on. Can you imagine the expense, just to build the stables? You can see their motif on the wall."

Oran had noticed the large letter C and the date 1830 marked out in black bricks on the wall outside the building in which they stood.

"This is where the servants lived up over the stables. It's a shambles but I want a place of my own. A studio..." Her voice wasted into silence. Turning away from him, she bent to pull a cobweb off the window-pane. A homeless spider scurried for cover. "Look!" she straightened up and pointed out the window. "Our land extends around the house. Most of it is leased out to a farmer but Richard was determined to buy. He said he wanted to bring the land back into Catholic hands where it belongs. Before the Corboys owned it, the land belonged to the O'Flahertys but they got run off it, of course. He takes it as a personal insult. Richard's mother was an O'Flaherty but we were never able to trace any connection. She..." Jane O'Molloy faltered. The confidence that she had displayed in the kitchen was all played out. Oran said nothing. Abruptly she turned and patted her hair into place, a middle-aged gesture that slotted her into the role of employer. "When can you start?" she asked.

"Would the beginning of next month suit you, Mrs O'Molloy?" He couldn't believe the note of servility in his voice. "I've a few weeks left in the college."

It was like a game that they were playing, switching back and forwards, in and out of roles.

She surprised him with the warmth of her response, her smile cracking open the matronly guise. "Oh, super!" she gushed. "Really super!"

Was it genuine or simply cocktail charm?

Out in the courtyard she was about to speak when they was distracted by the sight of a man coming out of the house towards them. A rounded, greying man in his forties, his hair smoothed back from balding temples. He wore a mohair suit, and carried a pair of leather driving gloves in his hand. His air of possession was that of a husband and when he reached them, the way that Jane touched his sleeve seemed to confirm Oran's impression that he was meeting Richard O'Molloy. Again she surprised him. "Meet our local TD, Oran." she said, her eyes smiling up into the face of the visitor. "This is Garret Heaney."

So this was the man that Fergus was up against. If Oran were a betting man his money would go on this horse. Garret Heaney looked the type who could eat boys like Fergus for breakfast. Up close, his sleek bonhomie was contradicted by his blocky hands and by his sharp, inquisitive eyes. Garret Heaney had the practised smile of a parish priest. He grasped Oran's hand, then dropped it fast. Oran felt peremptorily dislodged. Jane's hand coming close after was warm, less dismissive but its message was equally distinct. The interview was over. Oran looked around for an exit and to his relief, found one. Not far away from where they stood there was a open gate in the wall surrounding the courtyard. Beyond it, a gravel driveway, shaded by tall trees, lead away from the front of the house.

As he walked down the driveway towards the road, Oran had another encounter. A man wandered across a field towards him and ducked under a wire fence to join him. Richard O'Molloy was tall and fair, with a face the shape of a pear. He had a rosebud mouth and indented upper lip that, along with the flat heavy eyebrows and pale eyes rimmed with white lashes, gave him the look of an amazed schoolboy. He had what Oran's mother called a Protestant walk, all swaying hips and stiff charmless legs. He seemed unsurprised by Oran's explanation for his presence and cordially shook hands with him. "Well done," he said abstractedly and then he paused as if he were about to say something more. But instead, he waved Oran on his way before resuming his slow journey towards the house.

In the bank there was a queue of people and Oran had to wait his turn. As he took the fiver from the cashier he bitterly regretted his weakness. He was tempted to pocket the money and spin Dominick's wife some yarn. Through the window, he had seen her standing on the pavement. He didn't know why he had his urge to keep her waiting in the street. Something about her made him cruel. She was a natural victim and her lack of resistance riled him.

Outside, there she was, waiting to pounce. Her thin face could have been pretty once, but any sweetness had been squeezed out of it. She was stranded in a slum, her children dragging her down, while Dominick was off dreaming dreams and scheming schemes. Small wonder she couldn't compete with Cathleen Ni Houlihan for a place in those dreams. Anyway, there were too many bloody dreams for Oran's liking, and not enough action. He hadn't the nerve to fob her off. Silent and resentful, he stood and watched as the five-pound note disappeared into her pocket. Her little birdlike fingers almost snatched it out of his hand.

"I'll pay you back, I will. It's only to tide me over. For the kiddies' sake. I'll manage once they're all right."

Her eyes darted about wildly. She made no attempt to move but stood rooted on the pavement, her hand twisting inside her pocket so that the cheap material of her coat gathered into a bundle at her hip. Oran stared at the hidden movement of her fist, turning and folding under the cloth and calculated how many pints he could have bought with that fiver. He would never get his money back.

"Don't…" He felt the small tense grasp of her fingers on his arm. "Don't…"

Her expression was one of desperation. The bones of her face spoke while the mouth sang dumb, the bruises around her eyes deepening into ugly purple blotches.

Don't, he could have finished the sentence for her, let Dominick know. But he said nothing. The unsolicited intimacy and the exposition of her terror embarrassed him and made him angry. Keep Dominick out of this, he wanted to say to her, Dominick was above all this. She had his money, what more did she want? He would have liked to wrench her hand off his sleeve, but he hadn't the nerve to make a move. Of its own accord, her hand slipped off his arm. A sense of relief enveloped him and without thinking, he gave his jacket a brisk wipe.

She began to weep. The cry issuing between her lips seemed to shock her as much as him. A skinny, repressed sound that was excruciatingly painful like the shriek made by nails across a blackboard. She tried to subdue the sound, her spindly hands tugging at her face, but her suffering spilled out beyond any boundaries that she was capable of erecting. Tears poured down her cheeks.

Aghast at the sight of the crying woman, Oran stood rooted to the spot. At last she gave a shuddering sigh and lifted her hand to wipe her nose on her sleeve. Without a backward glance she turned and walked down the street, pushing her way blindly through the lunchtime crowds.

Outside the office where she worked, Marie was waiting for him. Seeing her, Oran was overcome by a sudden rush of affection. She stood, lost in thought, as she gazed into a shop-window. Inside the plate-glass window, plaster mannequins pouted above billows of white tulle and lace. He touched her shoulder and she turned to him and smiled.

"Aren't they beautiful?" she asked.

Wedding dresses! For a moment he stared, in bafflement, at the ghostly figures in the shop-window. Then he laughed, a loud braying laugh that turned heads around in the street. Hurt and surprised, Marie frowned at him.

"I need a drink," he said, no longer laughing, and steered her towards the pub.

At the entrance to the pub, there was a pool of liquid that had been accidentally spilt across the steps. It was some chemical, viscous and dark, that oozed across the concrete pavement. *Help me.* Involuntarily he closed his eyes. The sight of the liquid on the ground reminded him of Dominick's wife standing in the street, her hand clawing inside her pocket, while her life's blood trickled away into the drains.

"You'll be paying, love," he informed Marie. She sighed and opened up her purse and took out a ten-shilling note. Then a blush of delight spread across her face as Oran leant over and clumsily planted a kiss on the side of her mouth.

FIFTEEN

In the lounge of the pub Oran recognised a familiar face. To meet again so soon after their interview was out of the question. Swiftly he steered Marie towards the bar and out of sight. She protested at the bare floor and hard stools but Oran refused to sit in the lounge, no matter how comfortable the seating, and be the subject of his future employer's scrutiny.

Jane O'Molloy was unaware of Oran's brief appearance in the lounge. She settled into a corner seat and ordered lunch. A cheese sandwich and a bowl of oxtail soup. When it came, the bread was like cardboard and the soup a glutinous mess. Why is it, she wondered, that we accept food in a pub that we wouldn't feed a dog in our own homes? The old joke about fidelity: why eat hamburger out when you can dine on steak at home? Jane wished that life could be like that for her. How simple it would be!

Jane was haunted by the thought of Madge discovering the truth about her. That fear made her ever attentive to the other woman's needs. She offered to share school runs and they took turns to mind each other's children. But she could never like her. In Jane the two streams ran parallel, contempt and deference, each cancelling the other out. She maintained her stolid fetching and carrying as a constant reparation for the illicit alliance she enjoyed. But her dislike for Madge remained pure and uncontaminated by pity. As for Madge, no-one could say what she thought of Jane.

When Madge arrived she stood in the doorway and looked tentatively around the pub. She was a thin woman with a taste for pastel twinsets and scarves artfully draped at her neck. Straight dark hair weighed unflatteringly on her shoulders. Hers was a vaguely bohemian look that was marred by a spinsterish caution.

"How is the house?" she asked as she settled in beside Jane.

"Oh, you know old houses," Jane answered. "When you're finished one job, another starts demanding attention. You can see for yourself when you come to dinner tonight."

"You should ask Garret about getting a grant. I'm sure he could help you."

"Maybe," Jane said mischievously, "I should go down to one of his clinics and talk to him about it."

Madge giggled. "Don't be daft. Ask him tonight. I'm sure he could sort out something in the Department. He'll be going up to Dublin this week even though the Dáil isn't in session."

Will he indeed? Jane made a mental note. Not so long since they were both up in Dublin and it hadn't been grants they had been discussing. Jane leant back in her seat and closed her eyes to block out the sight of Madge's earnest face gazing into hers.

She withdrew into a world of her imagination like a bird tucking its head under its wing. The way Garret did sometimes. He could switch off in mid-conversation and he would no longer be there. Physically he was there, but that was all. The real Garret would be somewhere she couldn't reach. In bed he had a habit of suddenly falling asleep without warning and she would find herself talking into mid-air. There was a touch of a domestic animal about him like a cat dozing on a windowsill, or a dog curled up by the fire. As she watched him sleep a feeling of tenderness swamped her. It was different to anything she had ever experienced. When she and Richard made love there was always a reserve, an awkwardness persisting, no matter how often they lay down together. The involuntary start of surprise at the strangeness of his lips when they touched hers. Did she not love Richard, she asked herself, aware of a fear lurking deep in her bones. But no explanation fitted that unexpected phenomenon. Richard was her husband. They had stored up enough intimacy to forge a hundred marriages. Yet, with Garret, inscrutable, enigmatic, life and soul of the party, ebullient Garret she found there were no barriers. Or, if there were, she slid through them like a fish through a net. It frightened her. When words stumbled out of her mouth she had no control over what they signified. Love...agony...sweetness...darling. While at her household chores she would suddenly stop, eyes widening with shock at their recollection and yet, despite the abandonment to passion, she did not know Garret. While Garret, it appeared, knew her very well.

His estimation of her was accurately pitched. By spelling out his allegiance to the sanctity of family he was able to subvert any resistance that she might have presented. Jane had been up in Dublin for a few days selecting curtain fabric for the new house. Give me a call when you're next in town, Garret had said, his eyes resting a moment too long on her. So she had, nervously and trying to sound casual. "I thought, a drink maybe?" On the phone he had sounded so pleased, like a little boy, and insisted that they have dinner together. Halfway through the steak tartare she realized that both of them had intended for him to seduce her.

"My family are very precious to me," he had begun with disarming frankness. "It's not my style to run after some silly secretary. Too dangerous for one thing. She could be on the phone the next day, spilling the beans to the wife. Or to the newspapers. You're different. I can admire you and Richard, truly."

She had laughed. He basked in such an aura of well-being. No-one who was so cheerful could possibly be bad. Not really bad. He smelt of aftershave and cigar-smoke. She enjoyed Garret's ambition and admired his success, but his suits were a little too tightly-cut, his shoes too highly polished, his political strokes too blatant to be taken seriously. His vulgarity she found reassuring.

When they got up to leave, his hand brushed intimately across her leg. How obvious! she had thought. His eagerness made her feel superior and that confidence served to excite her all the more. Garret was an eminently suitable person for her adventure: discreet, attractive and too crass to be a danger. She had slipped and tumbled into his arms, thinking herself in control and able to bail out when she chose. But in bed, he conquered her. His body moved adroitly between the sheets, sensing her needs before she was even aware of them, surprisingly delicate in his love-making. Shaken, she had gone home to Richard swearing to herself that it would never happen again.

But, of course, it happened again. And again. Like someone starving between mouthfuls of food Jane embarked on her odyssey from one illicit assignation to the next. On the surface of her existence there was no hint of a disturbance. As always the ice-maiden presided over the household hearth. But in another world of hotel bedrooms and at grabbed moments, she burned in an unholy fire.

"What do you think is best, Jane? It's so hard to

know."

"Hmm?"

Madge was unaware of Jane's inattention and carried on. "How can you tell which is best? That's what I'd like to know. The national school was good enough for me."

Jane caught up with her. Education, the never-ending concern of the upwardly mobile. "Then send him to national school," she said.

"But look at the size of the classes!" wailed Madge. "How is a child supposed to manage? And Garret Owen is no Einstein. It's up to us to give him the best start in life."

"Then send him to a private school."

"But is it the best? You hear stories..." Madge stopped, overcome by the middle-class terror of being conned out of money. Jane smiled reassuringly at her. Garret Owen, it went without saying, was home and dry. In time, a place would be bought for him at Clongowes or Glenstal and a place reserved in university after that.

"Maybe you should keep him at home and teach him yourself, Madge."

"Oh Jane," Madge giggled, "you're no help to me at all!"

Later Jane stood up and said goodbye. Lunch hour was over and the pub was emptying.

"I'll see you tonight," she said, "Eight for half-eight. Carol and Ken are coming to dinner as well, it'll just be the six of us."

She stopped and looked down at Madge and wondered. Garret and Madge. Did he love his wife. Did he love Madge, dowdy and plain and predictable Madge? Love and marriage were mutually exclusive, said the cynic in Jane. Marriage was the grinding of millstones, the meshing of ratchets; marriage was the scaffolding designed to shore up old age.

SIXTEEN

In the drawing-room, Carol leant forward and selected a salted cashew-nut from a bowl on the coffee table. "On my holidays," she said, "I prefer my landscape to be of pools rather than peninsulas." As she spoke she pressed the cashew-nut firmly between her teeth. Jane sighed. There were times, she decided, when her sister was a pretentious windbag. Invariably, when Carol made her obscure allusions, she pouted as if she were making a risqué joke. It was an affectation that infuriated Jane but she refused to be defeated by it. *Peninsulas*. A reference, no doubt, to Carol's husband. Kenneth the Meek. A fortnight in Kilkee and the meek shall inherit the earth. In the unpromising setting of a rented holiday house Ken's sexual energies were known to blossom. Hard lino floors and comfortless furniture seemed to spark off a response in him that had the bedsprings pinging like a trampoline on wet summer afternoons, while the children played beyond the closed bedroom door. Carol had no scruples about giving Jane what she maintained were the tiresome details.

An evening sun burst through the tall windows

and illuminated the scene in the drawing-room: the two women seated on a sofa beside the fireplace and across the room, standing in a window alcove, their husbands deep in conversation over their whiskey glasses. Before the sun slid behind a trail of cloud, it lit up the room, the mahogany and plush inflamed by the sudden light. Jane's spirits rose. When she prepared for guests, positioning bowls of flowers in dark corners or angling a lamp to heighten its effect, she was conscious of a conspiracy at work. She and the house were in collusion; the rooms blooming under her ministrations and they, in turn, thrilling her by their beauty. Environment moulding personality. The architect in Richard was right about that much, at least. She would have said, if anyone had asked her, that instead of becoming owned by her, the house had claimed her. She wanted to merge into it, to become part of the furniture. No. Furniture could be too easily displaced. She wished to become an element in the structure; a wall or a spandrel or a roof-truss. Sometimes, she had an urge to lick the plasterwork until it was wet with her saliva, or to crouch in the overhang of a mantelpiece.

She stole a glance at Richard across an acreage of dun-coloured carpet. It was so right for the drawing-room, that carpet. His choice, of course. Sometimes she hated Richard for his perfect taste.

"You'll enjoy the break." Jane returned to the

conversation. She grinned manically at Carol to show that she had made sense of her reference to peninsulas. "You know what they say about a change and a rest."

"A rest," Carol rejoined, "is miles better than a change."

Jane noticed then how pale Carol looked. "Aren't you feeling well?" A euphemism if there ever was one. Not a fourth on the way, surely?

"I've never been better." Carol shook her head impatiently. "It's just that I've given up wearing make-up."

Peering at Carol's sandy-coloured lashes and open pores Jane wondered aloud, "Whatever for?"

"I refuse to pander any longer to men's perception of us as painted dolls." The reply deliberately loud. Bait for the men. Across the room, Ken rolled his eyes.

"But I don't wear make-up to suit men." Jane's fingers flew defensively up to touch her cheek. "I do it to suit myself."

"Oh yeah?" Carol said rudely. "You mean to tell me that you torture poor animals to death in laboratories, then clog up your pores with cream and powder, darken your lashes, lighten your hair, shave your legs, or worse, suffer the agonies of a leg-wax, gum up your finger-nails with polish, pluck your eyebrows and pull stray hairs out of your nose because it suits you?"

Jane giggled. "Well, it may sound silly but I'd feel worse if I didn't."

"Exactly!" Carol replied. "It's a guilt trip laid on women by men and I've decided I'm not playing."

Richard crossed the room. He stopped at the sofa and, leaning over Carol's shoulder, he filled up her glass from the bottle of sherry that he held in his hand.

"And you still look gorgeous!" he grinned and straightened up. Delicately he wiped the neck of the bottle with a white napkin that he carried draped on one shoulder.

Carol gazed up dreamily at him. "Fuck you too, Richard," she said.

The arrival of Garret and Madge Heaney was an excuse for Jane to banish the unwelcome vision that had flowered in her imagination. A vision of Carol with hairy masculine legs like those of old country women whom, as children, she and Carol used to make fun of, as they pulled up their flower-patterned skirts to sun themselves on the promenade at Salthill. Good God, Jane recoiled, Carol couldn't be serious!

Madge Heaney dived for safety into the haven created by Carol and Jane. Until dinner the pattern, now established, would be unchanged. Two hermetic worlds moving in their orbits; one revolving around domestic elements—children, husbands, food, the cost of shopping—and the other one, the male world whirling on an axis of business and sport and money.

"Oh, I do like your hair, Jane," Madge wailed. "I wish I could get mine looking like that."

Jane repressed her exasperation. She wondered yet again how Garret had married a woman so lacking in self-esteem. It was possible, she conceded, that she was being unfair to Madge. Living with Garret could have made her what she was; an ineffectual, self-abasing woman who was incapable of producing anything other than banalities into the conversation. Or maybe it was the security of her limitations that had attracted Garret in the first place. Madge would never threaten him—or anyone—with initiative, or wit or cleverness. If this was the wife, Jane thought and the thought deadened her, what did that make the mistress?

Between the three women, they had produced nine children so there was no danger of running out of conversation. As she listened to Carol and Madge talking babies, Jane was conscious of another thread of conversation tangential to theirs. Eagerly, she strained to hear what the men were talking about. She was certain that they had some secret advantage, a hidden vein of interest that would manifest itself if she looked hard enough.

"Playing any golf these days?" Richard was asking Ken.

"No chance," Ken complained. "The back has been giving me hell for weeks now. Anyway the last time Garret and myself went with Dineen, the bastard sprayed his shots all over the eighteenth."

"Dineen can go screw himself," Garret spoke into his glass, "if he ever comes looking for another game from me."

"What's the diagnosis, Ken?" Richard asked.

"I was back in hospital with it," Ken said plaintively. "It's pure hell. The medics say I have a condition called cervical deterioration."

"Christ, you'd want to watch that," Garret said in mock-horror. "Isn't that the disease that the nuns get?"

As Jane turned back to the women she caught sight of Carol. A knowing, ironic smile flitted across her sister's face. *Bo-ring, bo-ring,* Carol's expression said to her, clear as a bell, across the coffee-table. Jane shrugged and looked away. Who was Carol to talk, she thought unreasonably. She felt depressed by the sight of her pasty-faced sister propped up like a fat doll in the squashy upholstery of the couch. Where were they all heading except towards more of the same? Only worse; children growing up and abandoning them to afternoons of silence in vacant drawing-rooms. To bridge-parties, for Christ's sake. Afraid of the direction her thoughts were taking her, Jane switched tack. She looked again to the men for succour.

Garret Heaney sat angled away from her, so there was no danger of their eyes making contact and she was at liberty to examine him. He was huddled down between Richard and Ken, deep in the telling of a story, like a farmer sitting over a pint in a pub, his blocky hands spread out on his wide-apart knees. Every detail was distinct—the hairs curling on the backs of his hands, the half-moons of his manicured cuticles. The hands of a newly-made man, unable to bury their peasant origins, while pinkly displaying an acquired middle-class fastidiousness. Suddenly there was nothing else in the room except his fingers. They moved along her body, with a delicacy that those stubby knuckles could not denote, and drew the straps of her bra along her arms. They brushed against her shoulder-blades and, as they fastened the catch, dug against her backbone. While he clothed her slowly and methodically, she had sat on the hotel bed, unresisting. In the act, a memory was dredged up from her childhood; a recollection of her father dressing her as a child after a swim in the sea. Those same big safe hands travelling confidently over her body. And as she remembered, emotion had caught in her throat. "I've been undressed by a man before being bedded," she had laughed lightly, trying to dismiss it as a joke, "but this is the first time I was ever dressed by a man after being bedded." Then, unbearably moved, and anxious to prevent him witnessing her emotion, she had bent her head over Garret Heaney's cupped hand and had kissed the fingers that now, in her drawing-room, lay heavy and motionless upon his knees.

"Why don't you come with me?" Jane became aware of Carol's face close up, questioning, waiting for a reply.

"What?"

"Why don't you come with me?" Carol repeated.

"Where to?" she asked.

"The Women's Lib meeting in the uni. It'll be fun, Jane. Come on, give it a go."

Jane knew what Carol was after. Her sister wanted moral support but Jane had no intention of giving in to her on this one. Women's Lib indeed! "Oh Carol!" Jane laughed at the very idea. "You'll end up in trouble one of these days."

By the time she served up the meringue surprise they were all drunk—except Ken, of course. Carol's husband didn't drink but sat as usual, blinking behind his glasses. For as long as she had known him, Jane had never been able to unearth the hidden wealth of intelligence that was promised by those owl's eyes.

Across the table Richard and Garret were arguing. "You don't have any political philosophy," Richard said triumphantly. "You're a true naif when it comes to politics."

"Ah nooo..." Garret slyly resisted him, his forehead crinkling with concentration, "I'll tell you...since you keep asking me...I'll tell you what my political philosophy is."

"Well?"

"It's a good sound one," Garret continued, pulling on his cigar and refusing to be hurried. "A simple one for a simple man." He ignored Richard's snort of laughter. "Never do a man a bad turn. That's it in a nutshell. Here I am in a position to do a bit for someone, maybe yourself or a brother of yours. Not much I admit, but a word in a minister's ear, a grant maybe, a little job somewhere in the civil service. You're lucky to have me. I do the work. Old Cadogan did nothing in his day only collect his expenses."

"Tell me," Richard drawled. "When was the last time you spoke at a Dáil debate?"

"Have sense, man." Garret threw up his hands in dismay. "Sure, what would I have to say? Anyway you only lose votes by having opinions. I'm for Galway and Galway knows it and that's all about it."

"And you never look further than the parish-pump?"

Garret shrugged.

"What about the national interest?" Richard persisted.

"What about it? Isn't it doing nicely without me meddling in it? Listen, did I tell you about Lehane? The gobshite was asked in the Dáil about drainage in the western region. He started speaking, and it was only when he was halfway through his answer, that he realized that he was talking about a different county, altogether. And would you credit it? No-one noticed only himself that he'd been talking about Longford to a Leitrim deputy." Garret threw his head back and laughed. "The deputy was none the wiser and I've no doubt he went home and made a few farmers in his constituency happy with his news and where's the harm in that?"

"It's just a big game to you." Agitatedly, Richard ran his fingers through his hair. It sprang up in an angry orange aureole around his ears.

"Not at all," replied Garret. "It's a deadly serious business. I've a seat to look after. Cadogan still has his son there as the boy prince and the old hoor would like to see me topple the next time. He never forgave me for squeezing the young pup out at the convention. It's my own that I have to watch out for rather than the other crowd. Although the Labour men don't like him. If I can keep them sweet they'll come up with the transfers and we'll be in business forever."

"I would have thought your industrial troubles might have strained your relations somewhat with the Reds." Richard's eyebrows were arched in amusement.

"Yerrah, get away out of that! Those lads were scared shitless when my workers voted for a strike. A little pink about the gills, that's all those Labour men are. A few of them are rosy intellectuals, just enough to deliver me the university types in the new estates.

I look after the council estates myself. I'm the man the poor people come to when they need help. They don't forget me either when it comes to election-time." Garret stretched back on his chair and blew a circle of smoke at the ceiling. He lifted his glass and grinned around the table.

"It's an absolute disgrace," Madge said loudly. Madge was not given to making strong statements. Her interjection was sufficiently unexpected to stop the conversation around the table. Intrigued, Richard turned towards her. She sat, bolt upright in her chair, looking ferocious.

"Those strikers are holding Garret up to ransom," she stuttered. "They are nothing but troublemakers, out to destroy him. They should be sh-shot for what they're doing." Her face was blotchy and red from passion and wine.

Fleetingly, Garret touched her shoulder. It was a gesture of warning.

"No-one can break me, dear," he said gently, his hand companionable still on her arm. "I have my own way of doing things. The men are being greedy and acting thick at the moment but they're a bit like children. In time they'll come to their senses. If you show them firmness they appreciate it."

Madge sat back on her chair and looked as if she were about to burst into tears. Garret turned again to Richard and was about to continue speaking when suddenly Carol cut across him.

"Troublemakers...children," she mimicked. "Jesus, Garret, you are full of crap. Do you think we're idiots? Anyway, those guys are more than a match for you, laddie." She paused and then asked, "How many weeks are they out already— seven, ten?"

"Seventeen weeks and two days," squeaked Madge. "It is sh-shameful."

Carol ignored her. "You're living in the twentieth century, Garret. Isn't it about time you started acting the part?"

Garret smiled and, content to stay silent, blew another funnel of cigar smoke into the air. A tiny pause and then Madge spoke. "Money, money, money," she complained, although no-one seemed to be listening. "Those people don't understand that money doesn't make you happy. It's all they ever think about."

Carol quivered like a gun-dog on a scent. She turned her attention towards Madge. "I have always found," Carol said deliberately, "that sentiments about the evils of money are invariably expressed by people who have buckets of the stuff."

Her comment earned her an unexpected guffaw of approval from her husband. Ken had said nothing during the conversation. Now he sat back in his chair, his laugh dying as suddenly as it had erupted, and he bit into a peach. Still smiling broadly, he leant forward again to take a large carving of cheese from the cheese-board. Oh, help yourself, thought

Jane crossly, why don't you?

Ken satisfied his greed with a furtive determination. Vast quantities of food disappeared down his throat. Despite the scale of his consumption, nothing ever succeeded in modifying his thinness and the gauntness of his face. There was the incongruity of Jack Sprat and his wife about Ken and Carol. Richard had a theory to explain Ken's eating-habits at dinner parties. He reckoned that when Carol and Ken were on their own at home, Carol simply forgot to feed him.

"Can't we talk about something pleasant?" Jane took advantage of the sudden lull, and smiled brilliantly around the table. No-one responded. Richard picked up a bottle and dug the bottle-opener deep into the cork. Carol rested her chin in her hands while Ken munched contentedly on the Gorgonzola.

"I can never understand why people want to join a trade union." Garret said in his fruity, relaxed voice. Jane sighed in defeat and began to collect up the dirty dishes.

"You see, Carol," he turned to her and continued, "there isn't much point in having rights without responsibilities. These workers don't actually own anything themselves so they think they can afford to be reckless with other people's property. That's why I think of them as children. If they had a stake in life they'd be a lot slower to down tools. They own nothing, not even their houses."

"If they were paid decent wages they might."

Garret shook his head sorrowfully. "I only wish that life could be so simple. If I paid them more I'd lose my competitiveness. They would save themselves a lot of trouble if they simply faced up to the facts of life."

"They'll never give in," Carol said shrilly. Standing up in order to carry a pile of dishes out to the kitchen, Jane looked with surprise at her sister's flushed, angry face.

"How do you know what they'll do?" she wanted to know.

Carol looked mysterious. "I just know."

"You're being taken in by all the propaganda," smiled Garret. "In a situation like this you'll always get political activists trying to cause trouble."

"I wouldn't call Mrs Kinsella's husband an activist," Carol said. "Mrs Kinsella says that he isn't in the least bit political and that all he wants is to join a union."

Innocently Garret gazed around the table. "Well, well," he said. "It's the charladies we have to listen to now. Carol's daily help is advising us on industrial relations, may the Lord sustain us. I think you should tell your Mrs Kinsella and her little man that they're out of their league."

Carol said flatly, "They'll all stick together. The men will win through."

Garret tapped his cigar-ash onto his saucer. "It's a childish business."

Infuriated by his condescension, Carol lost her temper. She slammed her fists down on the table. "You're going to have to meet them," she shouted, her face contorted with rage. "When are you going to cop on and do a deal?"

"Carol! There's no call for you to..." Madge's tearful voice rose and collapsed.

"You're beaten!" Carol taunted Garret.

Thoughtfully, Garret raised his glass of wine and held it against his lips. Without drinking, he looked over the rim at Carol as he appeared to assess her challenge. His expression was almost coquettish, wide-lipped, beaming with good spirits. "Before I do a deal with that rabble..." He paused languorously. He could have been making her a promise, a covenant between intimates, the way he looked at Carol, his gaze following the curve of her neck down to her breasts pressing against the white tablecloth, while his eyes glowed warmly in the candlelight. The weight which he gave to the words leant them the solemnity of a commitment. "Before I do that, my dear Carol," Garret smiled into her eyes. "I swear to you." Oh, how well Jane knew that look, and the words to match it (that you are my little love, my dearest sweetheart, my own...) His emphasis was deliberate. "I *swear* to you that I will close down the factory."

A silence followed his statement; a muteness washed out in the wake of his victory. From the corners of the room the darkness converged to threaten the light of the candles ablaze on the table. Carol looked down at her plate, her cheeks drained of colour. After the din made by their argumentative voices the absence of sound was frightening.

"Well," Jane cried brightly, determined to retrieve the party, "I think it's time we all had coffee." Her glance hop-skipped across their faces so that she would not have to make contact with the crumpled look in her sister's eyes.

Out in the kitchen Jane set out the china cups on a tray while she waited for the kettle to boil. She heard him come in to the kitchen and anticipated his fingers pressing through the silky material of her dress. "The fragrance of your body drives me crazy."

"Fragrance!" she turned and snickered into his shoulder. "How genteel! How refined! My body smells, stinks even..." Her voice dropped as her mouth sought out the tunnels of his ear. Drunkenly she crooned, "I love the fact that my body excites you. I want to know it gets a response." Her hand moved down across his crotch and she laughed in acknowledgement of the hardness she encountered. Abruptly she slipped out of Garret's arms, moving fast towards the steaming kettle, sensing rather than hearing the footsteps in the hall so that she was standing, cool and distant, pouring water into a coffee-pot when her husband opened the door.

"Jane, the bloody bottle-opener's banjaxed," Richard said as he walked into the kitchen. Obediently, she groped around in a drawer and handed him a corkscrew. Then, ignoring the two men, she bent over the tray and carried it carefully out of the room.

Later the voices of their departing guests sucked the last dregs of life out of the house. Jane stood and watched the cars disappear into the dark. She started to clear away the debris of the dinner-table. In the doorway of the dining-room Richard stood, his shoulder pressed tiredly against the jamb.

"Let's go to bed," he said, opening out his arms.

"In a minute." She circumvented his embrace and stooped to pick up the tray. "I have to clear up first."

He stood aside to let her walk past him. As she brushed near him, she felt the soft exhalation of his disappointment.

Later when she came to bed Richard was waiting. Wordlessly they made love and afterwards he lay back and sighed. "I just can't tell what you're thinking."

Along the far wall of the bedroom, the wardrobe reared up out of the dark like a policeman. Rapidly her thoughts teetered over the piles of clothes scattered on the floor. Then on to tomorrow's lunch and away from danger. "Nothing much, really."

Side by side they lay, face up, and looking at the ceiling. "I do love you, you know," she said. It sounded like something said across a counter. Lovely weather...How are all the family...nothing kind of talk.

"I know," he said gently. "It's just that you are so distant. Even when we're close it's as if you're locked into a world of your own." So. That much they had in common.

"I'm sorry," she whispered. He laughed. The sound of his laughter jangled through the quiet rooms. She liked the sound of it. It was the sound of a man who was undamaged, a whole man at ease with the limitations that life insisted upon.

"I love you too," Richard said.

SEVENTEEN

"Will it take the weight of the desk?" Hers was a rhetorical question. She and Oran stood in the middle of the floor and looked down the long empty room. The studio was bigger than he had realised and it had taken Oran some time to clear away the debris. Methodically he had lifted the rotting timbers and jettisoned them into the yard below. It was satisfying work, the regular lifting and carrying the planks, the gradual exposure of serried ranks of joists beneath, the sight of dark woodwormy flesh falling away as he peeled back the outer layer of the structure. Outside the sunlight profiled the cobbles and stained the brick walls to the colour of red ink. In the eaves, birds bickered.

"Or a piano?" Jane O'Molloy worried aloud.

Oran shrugged. A floor was a floor.

"What d'you think?"

She made him uneasy. She had a way of standing beside him in the studio when he least expected it. She didn't seem to be able to leave the place alone or to let him get on with his work. But once he got started, the job proved easier than he anticipated, a labouring job with no foreman breathing down his neck. The only problem was Jane O'Molloy who hovered around the studio like a bored child looking for someone to tease.

"Or an easel?" She sighed discontentedly.

Oran bent over his work. The next moment she was gone. Without saying a word she slipped out of the room and disappeared down the stairs. Although she was aware of Oran's resentment, Jane couldn't stop herself returning again and again to the room over the stables. The studio was a fixed point in her life, a place of hidden meaning, a private place.

"What are you going to do in that studio when its finished?" Richard wanted to know. "Which will it be, orgies or coffee-mornings?"

"Don't sneer!" she raged. Currents directed her life in this direction and that. Father, mother, husband, children, all contributed to the inevitable drift. Rocks, occasional and isolated, rose up out of the stream and then sank without trace under a wave of domesticity. The studio, she believed, held a significance for her that was, as yet, unrevealed. A lodestar. Alone in that echoing sunlit space she would find...

What would she find?

Jane drove through the entrance gates of the house at Bearna and turned the car towards Galway. Forced out by a restlessness she couldn't define, she wasn't even sure which direction to take. As she drove into the city her resolve took shape. An instinct led her towards Carol's house. Yes, she thought with relief as she drove around Eyre Square. The route was comfortingly familiar, through the city and into the housing estate made up of regular lines of houses with arched carports, climbing the hillside above Lough Atalia. It was a route that led to Carol who would understand. Even if Jane didn't.

EIGHTEEN

Carol looked a mess. She was wearing a dress with a gaudy Greek pattern, flounces around the hem, and a rope belt. As she stepped back to let Jane into the hall it was clear that there were visitors in the house. Jane frowned. She wanted to talk to Carol alone. As she grew older, Jane was learning to appreciate family more. Family couldn't shut the door in your face when you went looking for help. Help, for whatever reason. She couldn't tell why, exactly, but Jane knew that she had to get out of her own house before the walls started to move in on her. And so she had come, looking for comfort, only to find that strangers had taken up all the chairs in Carol's kitchen.

Usually any friends of Carol arrived in Minis or Renault 4Ls packed to the roof with children. The women let the children run around on the road while they sat in Carol's kitchen, drinking cups of coffee and smoking endless cigarettes. These three women looked like they couldn't drum up a decent car between them. As Jane walked into the kitchen the women looked up at her with interest. They were all in their late twenties or early thirties. Two of them could have been sisters, being roughly the same shape, with short legs and low-slung bodies and the same swelling hips. They differed only in colouring. One of them was sallow-skinned, with short dark hair sprinkled with grey. The second woman was pale and colourless, her hair pulled back into a pony-tail. She had a habit of baring her teeth in a peculiarly animal way that made her look like an anxious rat. She was called Naomi. Both of them wore jeans and dark, shapeless jumpers and rolled their cigarettes out of a shared tobacco tin. The dark one, whose name was Aoife, wore a badge on her jumper that said *Brotherhood Sucks*.

The third woman was strikingly different. Ron was tall with flowing auburn hair. She wore a shawl thrown carelessly around her shoulders. Her brightly-patterned skirt had a fringed hem that dipped around her ankles. Her face was long and beautiful and she spoke with a husky North of England accent. Aoife, Naomi and Ron. As they were introduced, Jane was the object of their long, unembarrassed stares.

"I wanted to ask you to make something for the cake-stall," Jane excused herself awkwardly. "You remember, Carol, I told you about the sale of work for the school."

"Wow," Ron drawled in a deep, sensuous voice. "Amazing!"

She rubbed her hair so that it fell becomingly onto her shoulders. Aoife and Naomi sniggered. Even Carol,

Jane noticed with annoyance, was smiling.

Naomi covered up her immensity of teeth. "Hmmmmm," she hummed nervously. "A sale of work, hmmmmm...an interesting concept, when you consider that what gets sold is never considered to be work at all. And yet, without this hidden labour, our economic system would simply fall part. Can you imagine," she suddenly giggled, "what would happen if women *did* start selling their work?"

"Oh, but it's nothing really," Jane said apologetically. "It's just for a few hours. Everyone finds it a bit of a bore but it's not too bad really. In fact sometimes it can be fun."

The small dark woman chortled. This one is Aoife, thought Jane trying to remember their names. Naomi and Aoife; Scylla and Charybdis.

Naomi continued to speak in a loud agitated voice. "Let us examine the proposition put forward by Carol's sister. A few hours work, a bit of fun...give that estimation to a time and motion study consultant and see what they'd come up with. Are you aware how many, hmmm, woman-hours go into a simple operation like a sale of work?"

"It's not just women who do it," Jane said and then remembered that the only man involved in this particular operation was the school principal and he had made it clear from the start that his role was going to be limited to the provision of a caretaker. "My husband will help out on the day," she remembered with relief.

"Oh, how kind of him!" Ron, the tall woman, said. Her gorgeous eyes brimmed with amusement. Jane blushed.

"That's what we're trying to achieve." Naomi the rodent turned to Carol who was sitting beside her. She had an air of someone who was explaining something to a willing but ignorant pupil, as if Carol had asked her a question to which she was now responding. "We have to question everything. Hmmmm..." She stopped for a moment as if she'd lost the thread of her thought and then hurtled on. "Our role at work...at home...and our sexuality..." Abruptly she altered the focus of her attention away from Carol and burned with a new intensity at Ron. But, from across the room, the beautiful woman chose to ignore her. Instead she sat back so that her head rested against the wall and blew a stray strand of hair off her cheek.

Naomi turned back towards Carol. "We have to discover how our sexual attitudes frame our subservience. Men are responsible..." she paused, frowning with concentration, "hmm, yes, we know that," she seemed to be having a private disagreement with herself, "but their weapons are far more subtle than we give them credit for. Men may be stupid and crass but we've got to remember that they have centuries of experience in domination. It is only now that we are beginning to organise and resist that oppression. It will take a lifetime to create new modes of living which will not ape masculine power structures. Our relationships have to be fair!" Naomi pounded her fist in the palm of her hand and wailed. "Fair and honest! Not the possession of the female by the male but a love between sisters." Again her eyes hungered for approval but Ron's attention slid away until it focused upon Carol's face.

"Without men altogether?" Carol asked, puzzled.

"Without men." Aoife answered instead of Naomi. As she did so, she stood up and walked over to the sink and threw her cigarette carelessly among the tea-leaves. "The answer lies in the humble test-tube," she continued crisply. " Science has provided women with the final solution to our reproduction."

Jane's eyes widened with astonishment. She looked from face to face, searching for a hint of laughter, but there was none to be found. They were deadly serious. There was something repulsive about these women, she decided. Not that she was prejudiced, of course. People had a right to their own opinions. And then the unwelcome thought sprang into her mind, that she was deluding herself and that really she was a mass of prejudices. Well, she had no objection to what these lesbians did in private. What did they do in private? Momentarily she was distracted by a vision of Aoife and Naomi and Ron rolling around together in a big double bed. Anyway, she told herself, whatever it was that they did, she mustn't mind as long as they didn't do it in the street and frighten the horses. In principle, she decided, she was opposed to prejudice and that was the important thing.

But it didn't mean that she felt any less uncomfortable in their presence. Even when the three women got up to leave, she felt that they were dismissing her as someone beyond redemption. Or else not worth redeeming.

"Ciao!" Aoife waved a vague hand in the direction of the kitchen sink.

"We have to head out," Naomi said abruptly, shaking hands with Carol. "Think about what we've talked about, sister. Remember you are responsible for yourself. It isn't possible to go on forever letting other people live your life for you."

Jane looked across the room. There was a meekness about Carol that surprised her. Her sister leant forward, listening intently to Naomi's words and nodded.

Then Ron stood up, her long hair glinting in the sunlight. Her skirt swung around her ankles with a tinkling sound as she glided across the room towards Carol.

"We all have to learn the hard way," she said. Her tone was soft and intimate, in contrast with the hectoring manner of the others. "We may not have the answers, but each of us has to make our own discoveries about life. Otherwise we are simply children doing what we are told. Girl-children instead of women." She hesitated and looked, suddenly anxious, into Carol's face. "Is that what you want to be?" Ron asked Carol.

Carol held Ron's hand and, looking up into the eyes of the tall, beautiful woman, she shook her head. Jane was conscious of the moment, of the bond forming between the two women, and she felt an urge to jump in and destroy it, there and then.

"Don't surrender your judgement to anyone, Carol dear," Ron said in her low, musical voice and brushed Carol's cheek with her lips, "and remember, we'd really like to have you." Naomi glowered at her shoulder. Her teeth were big and yellow like tusks. "Come on, Ron!"

"What did you think of them?" Carol asked Jane after the three women had left.

"I don't know," Jane said untruthfully.

"I think they're really challenging. I've never heard people talk like them before."

"Where did you meet them?"

"The Women's Lib meeting up at the uni. I told you about it the other night but you wouldn't come with me."

"Oh," said Jane loftily, "I can't take that sort of thing at all. I've seen Women's Libbers on the television and they have no sense of humour. Some of them are so tough you'd wonder if they were women at all."

As she spoke she looked down at the kitchen table. The remains of the meal were strewn around, and two empty wine-bottles stood in the centre of the debris. Automatically she began to collect up the dirty cutlery.

Carol looked evenly at her. "Some people," she said, "would call me tough."

"Oh, you're not like those women," Jane reassured her quickly, "you're not like them at all."

Carol laughed. "You don't understand," she said, folding her arms and puffing out her chest. "I'd like to be thought of as tough."

Miffed, Jane concentrated on picking up the dirty plates and piling them on top of one another. She scraped the food onto one plate before stacking the rest of the plates.

"Well," Jane said, "isn't it funny the way people, who say they're all for the equality of women, happen to be the ones who go off and leave you with the dishes to wash? That wasn't a very sisterly thing to do, was it?"

"Jesu Maria!" Carol threw back her head and swore dramatically, "washing dishes and goddamn sales of work. As long as there are women like you around, men have nothing to fear. You are just so bloody middle-class."

Did she mean middle-class or middle-aged? Jane stared at her sister and felt like bursting into tears. "You're absolutely right," she replied spiritedly. "I am middle-class. I'm a middle-class housewife and I'm not pretending to be anything other than what

I am," she paused and glared at Carol, "and just because you dress up like a peasant and won't shave your legs, sister dear, it doesn't make you anything else except a middle-class housewife either."

There was a moment's silence. Angrily the two women stared at one another and then, without warning, Carol burst out laughing. Her peals of laughter only served to infuriate Jane further. With ferocious concentration, she clattered plates and cutlery on the draining-board. "Oh, shut up," she said crossly. But Carol's laughter was infectious.

"Oh Jane," Carol spluttered, "did you ever think we'd end up like this?"

Jane bit her lip.

"Did you?"

Jane refused to give in.

"Glorified scullery-maids!" Carol said softly. "Glorified unpaid scullery-maids!"

Jane gave up all pretence and began to giggle. Was it funny, peculiar or funny, ha-ha? They could have been back at school, two schoolgirls in hysterics over some bit of nonsense and laughing until their stomachs ached. When they finally stopped laughing, it seemed pointless to clear up any more. Carol found a bottle of wine and put it in the middle of the table.

"Come on," she said. "I think the domestic staff are entitled to a drink." Elbows angled on the table, the two women sat and chewed on the leftovers of food with a carelessness that only long familiarity allows.

"Delightful cheesecake, Carol," Jane said, her mouth full.

"Why thank you, Jay darling," Carol said archly. "I'll let you have my delightful little recipe." That set them off again. The two women rocking back in amusement to watch themselves playing at being grown-ups and, for a moment, time was on the turn.

"Jesus, we haven't laughed like this for years!" Jane said.

Eventually they shared the dishwashing between them and Carol plunged the dishes into scalding water before Jane dried them.

"How's Ken?" Jane asked, not really caring how Ken was.

"He's getting worse," Carol replied. She dredged up a wine-glass from the hot water and stared at it. Then she stood the glass on the draining-board and put her hands down into the water again to fish around for another. "I didn't notice it at the start. He was just having an off-day or going through a bad patch. You try not to notice how he doesn't bother with the kids or what a goddamn whine he is. Jesus!" She jerked her hand out of the water, gripping the stem of the wine-glass in her fingers as if she were about to crush it. "Anyway, I just don't care anymore. I thought it was me but it's not. Ken has become a shrivelled-up, neurotic hypochondriac and he is killing me slowly but surely with his obsessions about his back and his stomach and his goddamn athlete's foot."

"Oh Carol," Jane said vaguely, "he's not that bad."

Briskly Carol rubbed her hands on the dishcloth and began to tidy the dishes away into cupboards. "First it was low back pain and he had a series of tablets and heat lamps and corsets and no sex for six months. Then it was his stomach and we had special diets and regular meals and more tablets. Then it was all in his head and the doctor told him sex would relax him so we had sex every night and morning until I had semen running out my ears and then he went into a religious phase when he thought God was some kind of witch doctor in the sky who would cure all his ills. Last month I ended up with him at a faith healer."

Jane laughed sympathetically. None of this was new to her. Carol had a tendency towards the dramatic. Tendency. Jane liked that word. It expressed the way Carol was always leaning towards disaster, never quite toppling over. Jane felt mature in comparison, sensible to her responsibilities.

"All men are a bit like children, Carol," she said primly. "Why can't you just humour him a bit."

"Humour him? I'm tired humouring him. I've been keeping him in fucking cotton-wool for years," Carol snarled at the dishwater. "Who has ever humoured me?"

Jane sighed. "You shouldn't curse like that, Carol.

Anyway, for as long as you've been married you've gone on about Ken. Just imagine if you were on your own! You'd have no-one to complain about then."

Carol stayed silent. She nibbled at her fingernail and stared out the window. In the garden a rotary line fluttered with a week's washing. Drops of rain spattered the window-pane. "Goddamn rain," she cried.

Together the two women ran out into the garden and unpinned the damp, flapping clothes. When they were finished, they came back into the house, their arms laden and their heads and shoulders speckled with raindrops. As they began to fold the washing on the table Carol continued to speak as if there had been no interruption. "He leaves the tops off all the jars in the bathroom. And the toothpaste so that it's running out all over the basin. He's a lazy sod." She picked up a man's vest. "Look at that. Do you want to know something about it?" Puzzled, Jane looked at the vest. "When I hang out the clothes," said Carol, "I always make sure that his underwear isn't hanging next to mine on the line. That's how much he gets to me. I can't even bear his goddamn socks beside mine."

Her grumbling was beginning to get on Jane's nerves. "Oh, for goodness sake, Carol." She flipped open a cigarette packet and offered her sister a cigarette. Outside the rain thickened. It splashed along the concrete path and swirled down the drain at the

back door. "Ugh," Jane said, "what stinking weather."
She leant across the table to light the cigarette for
Carol.

Carol ran her fingers through her hair. A silence
fell and then, "The sand grouse is about to fly to
heaven," Carol said unexpectedly. She breathed in a
mouthful of smoke and expelled it quickly. Jane
sighed with exasperation. Give me patience, she
thought. "And I am finally going to do something
about him."

"Oh, come off it," Jane said dismissively. "You've
been trying to change Ken for years. I think you
secretly enjoy having him to moan about."

"This time I mean it."

Jane glanced at Carol. Her sister avoided meeting
her eyes. It gave her a deceitful look, the way her
glance shifted uneasily about the kitchen.

"What on earth are you planning?"

"Aoife and Naomi and Ron have asked me to go
back to Dublin with them." Aoife and Naomi and
Ron. For a moment the comic ring to the trio of
names humanised them. Ooops, thought Jane, hu-
person-ised them. What on earth was Carol talking
about?

"For a visit?"

Carol shook her head impatiently. She pursed her
lips. Jane sat back in her chair. "Ron said I could go
and stay with her and Naomi for a while. Until I got
on my feet."

Jane heard herself speak, but someone else was forming the words, someone at the other end of a tunnel. There was no mistaking Carol's intention. Suddenly it felt as if a stream of ice was sliding down Jane's back.

"Ron just fancies you," she retorted. But if she had intended to put Carol off she hadn't been successful. Instead of being offended, Carol just looked at her as if she had said something interesting.

"Really!" she asked. "Do you think she does?" Piqued, Jane could think of nothing to say.

"This is the first time in my life," Carol emphasised each word as if she had made a momentous discovery, "that I have taken control of my life. Instead of letting things happen to me I feel I'm finally growing up." Gently she ground her fist into the palm of her hand. "Don't you see?"

Jane saw. Why didn't you exert your will when it really mattered, she wanted to say to her sister, instead of now when we're both trapped? What gives you the right to get out like you were someone with a special dispensation? It's all very well to talk about leaving but shit, Carol, where does that leave me? But Jane didn't say what she thought. Instead the words that issued out of her mouth were an automatic response.

"But you can't just leave a marriage because he doesn't put the lid back on the toothpaste. It isn't right. After all, you did marry Ken." Who was she to talk about the inviolability of marriage? Who the hell was she to preach duty? "Anyway," she changed tack, unwilling to go down that avenue of enquiry, "you'll never be able to manage in Dublin. Not with three children and no money to live on. It's just a crazy notion that those butch women have got going. They don't know anything about the real world."

"I know." Carol folded the last garment and carefully carried the pile over to the hot-press. The smell of newly-washed clothes filled the kitchen. It was a comforting domestic smell. It served to reinforce Jane's conviction that what Carol was saying was wrong. Right or wrong. Who knew any more? It was unsafe talk. Dangerous talk, that she knew. Carol's face was hidden by the hot-press door so that Jane almost failed to catch her words.

"I'm not planning to take the children with me," Carol said.

The words dropped into a silence. The kitchen clock hummed, the fridge clicked into action. Jane felt old. Older than Carol, older than the world. Carol was talking heresy. No mother left her children. No-mother-left-her-children. That was a cardinal rule, inviolate. Children were sacrosant. Jane lived by that rule and her faith in it was absolute.

"Now you're going too far!" Jane was furious again. "Who is going to look after them? I suppose you think I will. While you're off in Dublin finding yourself, this old eejit here will be left holding the babies. Christ, Carol, as if I didn't have enough to do."

"Thanks for the offer," Carol said dryly, "but I never said anything about you looking after them."

"Then who's going to?" Jane would have gladly stood up and shaken Carol until her teeth rattled.

"I think it's about time that their father looked after them."

Ken? Jane was silenced by this novel solution. Ken of the bad back and the bad breath. Ken who couldn't even look after himself.

"You're impossible, Carol!"

But her anger had dissipated as quickly as it had arisen. Miserably, she withdrew into silence and twiddled her thumbs in her lap while she tried to think of some other course to make Carol come to her senses. And yet, concurrent with her disapproval, she felt the stirring of a new emotion. A spurt of optimism. Someone, at least, was doing something.

"Oh Carol, are you just having me on?"

She found Carol's reply strangely reassuring. "I've never been more serious," Carol said. "This is going to be the beginning of the rest of my life."

Jane sat back and abdicated responsibility.

"I just hope you know what you're doing," she said. Carol said nothing. Jane noticed that her sister's eyes were pink-rimmed and puffy and she added quickly, "You don't look very happy about it."

Her comment sounded cold and judgemental. It

was the unwelcome sound of Mama's voice issuing out of her mouth. Carol collapsed down again beside her, her fingers worrying at the fringe of the table-cloth. She looked heavier than ever, like a tyre with a slow puncture overhanging the kitchen chair, her thighs huge in the Peloponnesian zig-zag patterned skirt.

"Oh Carol!" Filled with remorse, Jane wanted to console her and she gripped Carol's hand to calm the frenzied movement of her fingers on the fringe.

"Sometimes I think," Carol began to cry great sobs onto her sleeve, "that I'm too old to do anything about it. Too old and too fat and too craven." She lay her head down between her arms and wept.

"I'll come and see you," comforted Jane, "when I come to Dublin." Another excuse, she thought, to see Garret. Maybe with Carol in Dublin she might muster up enough courage to tell her about him.

"It's all right for people like you," Carol continued wetly into her sleeve. "You like marriage. You waltzed into it and never looked back. You were a little mouse until you got married. It's because you have a stable personality. You can fit into the pattern and it's plain sailing. Not like me."

Stable! Jane heard it as a sneer. If only Carol knew the half of it. The self-abasement, the crazed hours of waiting for a phone-call, or for the touch of his hand, or sitting in the visitors' gallery looking down on him, as he lounged, bored and half asleep, across the back benches. No-one knew, least of all Garret, how she grovelled for one iota of his attention. She was a bitch who enjoyed being kicked and came back with her stomach dragging on the floor, pleading for more. "How dare you say that I'm stable?" Her voice was loud and argumentative. "If you only knew..."

But Carol didn't know and wasn't interested. Which was fair enough, Jane supposed. After all, it was Carol's marriage that was in the process of falling apart.

So they sat there in the kitchen, while Jane listened and Carol talked until, through the window, they saw two children come around the side of the house. A boy and girl dressed in school uniforms and carrying their schoolbags slung on their shoulders. As they came under the roof of the carport the girl, who was the smaller of the two, suddenly lunged at her brother and whacked him across his ears. "You did it first," she yelled furiously.

"I didn't. I didn't."

"Mummy, Mummy, he did!" The girl slammed open the door. The boy was slower to rush in, made shy by the presence of Jane in the kitchen. Carol looked up to confront the rage in her daughter's face.

"I wonder, dear," she said thoughtfully, peacemaker now, "aren't there always two sides to every story?"

The little boy's face collapsed. His mouth opened wide in a howl of misery. Three pairs of female eyes rested attentively upon him. In the screwed-up eyes and tousled fringe of the little boy Jane recognized the doleful expression of his father. This was the face of Ken the Inconsolable.

Oh yes indeed, sister, thought Jane helplessly as she bent to touch the boy's warm wet cheek, two sides at least, and no Mama to sit in judgement and tell us right from wrong. Your story and mine, and Ken has his, and Richard too, and even Garret has a story, although God knows what it is. All of our differences tangled up together. And in the end, like Mama used to say, it is bound to finish up in tears.

NINETEEN

"Howya!"

It took Oran a moment to recognise Fergus. There was an air of confidence about the way he sauntered up to Oran. Almost a swagger. Oran hadn't seen him since that first meeting in the shed along the river and, uncertain what to expect, he nodded cautiously. "How's tricks?" he asked.

Fergus brushed back his fringe of pale hair and smiled. There was no trace of sullenness in his face. He was bursting with good humour. Oran stared at him. "Oh, for goodness sake," Marie muttered in his ear, but curiosity prompted Oran to pursue the conversation. "So how's it going?"

"We have Heaney on his knees. I'd give him two more weeks and he'll be ready to cave in."

This was news indeed. "Really?"

"Come on with me and I'll show you."

Marie grimaced. Her grip on Oran's arm felt like a dead weight but, intrigued at the transformation in Fergus's personality, Oran ignored her. The last time he had seen him in the shed, slumped in his chair, the boy had been pale and pinched and dejected. Now his face glowed and his shoulders, once hunched defensively, were jiggling with enthusiasm.

The three of them crossed the street and walked down towards the river in the direction of Nun's Island.

"Hundreds of typewriters we sent out of that place each week," Fergus said. "That's a lot of profit for Mr Garret Heaney not to be getting any more. And the place is full of stuff that hasn't budged since we called the strike. Heaney knows it's more than his life is worth to try and shift any of it. He's feeling the pain of it and he doesn't like it. Only the best of eating and drinking for Garret and keeping the builder's wife happy."

Marie giggled. Oran was puzzled.

"Aren't you up working in the house?" Fergus remembered. "You'd see what goes on. That man, the builder," Fergus persisted. "That architect," he said the word with ironic reverence. "Heaney and his wife."

"Is that right?"

Fergus flashed a grin at Oran. "They've been seen."

In front of the locked factory gates a caravan was balanced precariously on concrete blocks. At the open door a flag drooped.

"The old green, white and gold." Fergus looked at it admiringly. "I wonder where that came from?"

Inside the caravan, two men were playing cards. They lounged on the torn shabby seats that ran along each side of a narrow formica-topped table. Between them a transistor blared out pop-music. One was an elderly man, white-haired and toothless, who eased his way down the seat to give Oran and Marie space to sit down. Fergus slid in beside the other man, a stocky man in his forties, with heavy shoulders and a big belly.

"Well, Fergus," the man said, "you missed the crack."

Across the table from him, the white-haired man chortled.

"Tell us," said Fergus.

"I'm not right yet after it."

"Come on, what happened?"

"Earlier on today Paddy and myself were here on our own. When, all of a sudden, a car stopped outside, an old banger of a station-wagon, I'd never seen before in my life. And four big strangers got out." The stocky man paused. He eyed the window, as if the men were about to reappear. "Hold on, said I to Paddy, these must be Heaney's men."

The old man nodded. "Right enough they looked the part. Then one of them opened up the boot of the car real slow and brought out a load of piping."

The stocky man began to laugh. "When I saw what they had in their hands I think my heart stopped." His laughter was overtaken by a loud, hacking cough that had him bent double at the edge of the table. Noisily he cleared his throat. "Well, fuck this, says I," he continued, "we're in trouble now." Red-faced with embarrassment, he stopped short and turned towards Marie. "Begging your pardon, Miss."

Marie looked at him coldly.

"I never thought," he said, wiping stray spittle off his mouth, "that I'd be planning to die for this old factory but here goes, says I, and Paddy there along with me. For safekeeping, Paddy took out his teeth and put them up on the shelf. Just to be on the safe side."

The stocky man laughed. The sound was like the honking of a sea-lion. Marie bit her lip as Fergus grinned broadly at Oran across the table.

"Mother!" the old man said, his mouth gaping pinkly. "I forgot me teeth."

He stood up. His hand groped along the shelf above his head until he lifted down a set of false teeth. He dusted them carefully and then slipped them into his mouth.

"So there we were," the stocky man continued, "all set to die for Ireland. And the next thing the four boys screwed one length of piping onto the next, until it was one long pole. Jesus, we were praying! Paddy was hanging on to me and I was hanging onto him. And then..." He paused for effect as his companion rubbed his hands gleefully. "One of them steps up and introduces himself. He said they were an official delegation sent up from the Midlands trade union federation. A gesture of support, says he, and hands us up the pole with the flag on it, along with a cheque for twenty-five quid."

"For the strike fund," added the old man. Crowing triumphantly, he waved a cheque in the air.

Fergus took the cheque and examined it. He stood up and pinned it on a noticeboard that hung on the back of the door. There were cards and letters stuck up on it. Messages of support.

"When this is over," Fergus turned and looked at Oran, "we'll send it all on to Heaney, every letter to show him how many were with us."

And Oran understood why Fergus had brought him. Fergus wanted to drive the message home to Dominick and Brian about the strike. About how they were winning out, regardless.

As Oran turned away from the notice-board, something outside caught his eye. He squinted through the window and recognised the placard that Fergus had displayed at the Bloody Sunday rally. It was tied to the railings of the factory but now, although the numbers were still black and distinct against the white background, they looked different. Shabbier and different.

"Eighteen..." he wondered aloud. "What's that for?"

"That's how long we've been out," Fergus replied cheerfully, "Eighteen weeks, and if it takes another eighteen, we'll still be here, and another after that, if needs be."

The words sank into a silence. It enveloped the

group of people huddled in the cramped space of the caravan. No-one spoke. The men's expressions gave nothing away. They were impassive. A fortress of faces. Fergus stretched and said casually, "I had a visitor myself."

"Oh?"

"Dick Moriarty. Called to the house the other night."

"Father Moriarty to you, young fella." The old man straightened up and frowned across at Fergus. "Show some respect."

Fergus shrugged. The old look of sullenness shadowed across his face. "He wanted to talk to me, he said. At me, more like. About my duties and responsibilities. Heaney's a good employer, he said, and I shouldn't forget it. A decent Galway man."

The stocky man swung around sideways on the seat and spat. Marie flinched.

"Sure, he is only trying to help," the old man soothed. "There's no harm in that."

"He said worse." Fergus scraped his finger-nail on the formica. "He said that we had no business closing the factory. There's many before us as had to leave because they had no work. He kept asking me what did we do it for? Why are we sacrificing our jobs and families, he said, on this madness."

"Bejesus!" the stocky man said eagerly. "And I hope you told him."

A lopsided grin illuminated Fergus's face, "No

better man. I told him we have rights that are being denied us. I told him that the reason we did it was *for* our jobs and our families."

"And what did he say?"

"That's when he called me a communist. There, in the kitchen. Did you ever hear the like?"

Fear stabbed the stuffy atmosphere of the caravan. It was palpable in the changed expressions on the faces of the two men. Fergus chewed on his lip. His eyes darted across their faces.

The old man looked down at his fingers entwined on the table as if in prayer. "May God forgive him," he said simply.

"What did you say?" The other man leant forward. His face was drained of colour.

"I told him we weren't machines, I told him we were human, that's all. Nothing more and nothing less. And wasn't it strange, I said, that them foreign companies coming in can pay decent wages and treat their workers with respect when our own cannot, or will not, do the same."

The stocky man slammed his fist down on the table. "The very thing!" he bellowed.

In the old man's face, conflicting emotions competed for supremacy. He worried aloud, "D'you think he'll make a sermon on it?"

"And if he does?" Fergus answered him excitedly. "So if he does? We will stand together." He rolled his hand into a fist and pressed it down hard on the table. "And never fail. United we stand. We all voted for the strike, every man-jack of us. We made a democratic vote on it. That's for the record." He paused for a moment and looked around the caravan. His glance fell on Oran and he nodded slyly across at him. "You wouldn't have much experience of that kind of thing."

That struck home, as did the pride rippling through his every movement. What was the point in being a revolutionary, Oran asked himself, if he couldn't commit himself to a fight like theirs? He would play the part that Fergus had allotted him. He would carry back the message he had received. A courier like uncle Shamie had been. The only difference was that he would carry through his mission. He would keep his word. And if he had the words, Oran would have said as much. Maybe he was out of his depth but he still knew the direction to take. "I've got to go," he excused himself, "Dominick's expecting me."

Fergus jerked his head dismissively. "Still fighting ghosts, is he?"

Oran shrugged.

"There's real battles to be won," Fergus said. "For them that's not too blind to see."

Oran wondered at his air of authority. When Fergus flicked back the fringe of hair that hid his eyes, the contours of his face were exposed, and his face shone with an innocence, luminous and clear, without a whisper of guile. There was a hint of supplication in the way Fergus cocked his head to one side and waited for a response to his unstated question. Are you with us or against us?

Oran stood up and, self-consciously, stretched across the table to shake hands with the two men. "Beir bua," he said. He wished he could say more. He wanted desperately to promise something concrete, to make a gesture of some sort to show them where he stood. Wordlessly, he nodded at them.

Outside the caravan, the air smelt sharply of the sea and there were puffs of clouds scudding across the sky. From its vantage point on the railings, the placard loomed up at him. Below the freshly-made numbers, someone had painted a message in shaky black lettering. *Beware the Risen People!*

Marie tugged impatiently at his sleeve. "My goodness," she said and took a deep breath, "what a crowd of wasters! Not a window open in the place. I wonder what their wives think of them hanging round that caravan all day."

Furiously, Oran rounded on her. "What are you talking about? They're on strike!"

"I don't care what they are," she sniffed. "I wouldn't have anything to do with them." She almost shuddered. "Not with their BO."

Oran gritted his teeth. He opened his mouth to argue and then, abruptly, he changed his mind and strode on to the bridge that led towards the centre of the town. He was moving so fast that Marie had to run to keep up with him. Neither of them said a word until they came to the door of the office where she worked.

"Are you coming over tonight?" he asked automatically.

"I might," she answered him pertly.

Irritated, he dug his hands into his pockets and hunched his shoulders. It could go on forever, this cat and mouse business. He was tired of her and the way she kept tantalising him with promises. "Suit yourself," he said and turned on his heel.

A look of helplessness swept across her face as she stared after him. Beached so unexpectedly on the pavement, she made an incongruous figure, arms akimbo, mouth gaping with astonishment.

"I might..." she faltered, "Oran..."

Under the wiry cloud of hair, her eyes filled with longing. But he had walked out of earshot, and even if he heard her, he kept on walking.

Dominick and Brian were waiting for him. Under their weight, Brian's car sank so near to the ground that it looked like it could never get started again. But, as soon as Oran got in, the gears ground into action and the car moved away from the kerb.

"Bad news to be waiting round here," Dominick said.

"Sorry," Oran was humble. "I met Fergus." Dominick drummed his fingers on the dashboard and whistled thinly through his teeth.

"The strike is getting support." Oran felt awkward, unsure of the response his listeners might give him. "They're out now eighteen weeks and they reckon they'll be able to stick it out for as long as it takes."

"Is that a fact? " Brian waved his hand loosely out the window and then turned the car onto the main road out of Galway. Encouraged, Oran began to talk. He had just started on the story about the flag and the false teeth when Dominick interrupted him, leaning towards him, his face, stiff and tense.

"Is that the Branch?" he asked.

Oran turned in his seat and peered out the back window. Behind them, a car slowed down and turned off into a field. Dominick expelled a sigh of relief and sat back. Oran took advantage of his temporary relaxation. "They could do with some support," he said.

"So could we," Dominick replied through clenched teeth.

"But they're having a hard time of it." Conscious of his new-found sense of responsibility towards the strikers, Oran refused to give up until Dominick startled him by turning around again.

"We're carrying, right?" he spat the words out. "If we get caught we'll have a fucking hard time of it. Now keep your eyes on the road behind."

Shocked into silence, Oran twisted around in his seat to check the rear window. The road was clear but he remained vigilant, aware of the danger. *Why* were they carrying? He would have liked to ask but no-one asked questions like that. In this game, he had learnt, you did what you were told. Instead he concentrated his attention on the road behind. So much so, that when the car screeched to a standstill, Oran was unprepared and he was flung violently against the front seat. Brian switched off the engine and the three of them sat in stunned silence. For a moment, no-one did anything. Then Brian inched the car door open.

"Mother of God!" he exclaimed as he gazed in awe at the body lying on the road. "Where, in the name of Jesus, did that fella come out of?"

TWENTY

T he body was still alive. They could tell from the way the legs twitched.

"We can't leave him like this," Brian said. As if in response the body arched in a paroxysm of pain. Suddenly, without explanation, Dominick turned his back on Brian and walked away. He kept walking until he came to a gap in the hedgerow where he stopped to peer intently across the fields. "Only one thing to be done," Brian continued as if Dominick still stood beside him. "Oran, keep a look-out."

On either side, fields stretched away. Except for the figure standing at the ditch, the road was empty. Brian ducked in to the car and rummaged around under the dashboard. He reappeared, with tousled hair and a triumphant grin on his face. In his hand he waved a revolver.

"For God's sake," an agonised Dominick urged from a distance, "keep it out of sight."

Brian lifted the revolver and took aim. A sudden blast and the Alsatian kicked backwards under the impact. Then the dog lay still, bloody intestines spilling out of its shattered side. Mesmerised, Oran stared into the animal's eyes as Brian nudged it gingerly with his foot. The sound of footsteps startled them. It was Dominick. He spat into the ditch before he climbed back into the car. There was an odd, greenish tinge to his complexion.

"You know," he said at last, as the car moved off, "there's nothing I hate more than the sight of blood."

"A stupid fool of a dog," Brian grumbled. "I never saw him coming."

If the guards ever bring us in for questioning, Oran thought, it will be more likely for a driving offence than for any offence against the state. He glowered out the window. His comrades-at-arms were turning out to be a disappointment, a crowd of incompetents, not his idea of revolutionaries at all. MacIntyre was different. From the first moment that Oran had clapped eyes on MacIntyre he recognised that he was up against the real thing at last.

"Make sure your security's tight," Dominick had warned them that night. Edgy with excitement, they had stood around Brian's kitchen and waited for MacIntyre to come. Even the Branch had a welcoming committee; four men jammed into a blue Cortina stationed across the road. MacIntyre arrived on time. A blocky man in his forties with a reddish goatee beard, he was neatly dressed in a muddy green polo-neck under his dark suit. Except for his scuffed, out-of-shape shoes, he could have been mistaken for a businessman. Just by the way he sat in a chair, his presence in the room commanded respect. He took

Dominick and Brian aside. In response to some question he muttered at them, Dominick waved Oran over and for a moment, MacIntyre appraised the new boy, looking at him as if he were checking for faults before he bought him. Then he handed Oran the keys of his car.

"See if you can lose those bastards," MacIntyre said.

Accompanied by Kevin, all long legs and short cuffs flapping, Oran ran, head down, towards MacIntyre's car. He swung the car out into the traffic, watching for Moran's face to come into view. Out towards Salthill as if the devil was after him. Crouched down over the wheel he kept going, delirious at the sight of the Cortina straining to keep up. They stuck with him all the way to Bearna and he couldn't stop laughing at the brakes screeching and the tyres burning on the roadway when the Cortina swung around and sped back towards the city. It wasn't much of a victory but Oran felt a surge of satisfaction at having accomplished his goal.

His pleasure turned out to be short-lived, for when he and Kevin arrived back at the house the door was opened by Brian's mother.

"Where did they go?" Oran asked.

Out of a mist of incomprehension the old woman tried to focus on his question. "Is it the O'Grady boy with you?" Her gaze wavered over his shoulder. "Kevin O'Grady, surely?"

Oran tried again. "Did they tell you where they were going?"

A dribble of saliva eased down the side of her mouth. Her eyes widened and fixed on Oran. "Is it Brian you want?" Oran nodded. Was she just acting confused? It was impossible to know from those hard bright eyes of hers.

"He's gone to the shop for me cigs," she said and then she slammed the door in his face.

Oran hadn't the nerve to ring the doorbell again and he returned to Kevin who was sprawled in the passenger seat. "I suppose you've no idea where the meeting's set up?"

Inexpertly Kevin unstuck a wet cigarette-butt from his lip and shrugged. Oran crashed his fists against the steering-wheel. Christ, the first bit of action and he'd been left out of it. A decoy! That's all he was good for. He did everything they asked him. Sold the paper around every pub in Galway, made himself available whenever they asked. Not that much ever happened, even after they'd brought him into the movement. Training with broom-handles and taking oaths was meagre fare for him who had joined up to right a terrible wrong. He had committed himself to the armed struggle. He had done everything except write it in his own blood and they still didn't trust him. It was a wonder that gang of culchies let him join. Oran was reliable. Other people were always late or else they forgot to turn up for meetings and yet, for all that, his diligence seemed to make him suspect in their eyes. Even with the little responsibility that they gave him he had been determined to show them how good he was and now his reward was to be left out in the cold while, somewhere, the rest of them were making decisions.

"First we find Lar," Dominick was saying to Brian. The incident with the dog was forgotten and Dominick had recovered his usual jauntiness. "He'll be in the Ranchero. Then we'll find a quiet spot for the transfer. In and and out in a jiffy, like the bishop said to the actress."

A chuckle rumbled up from the depths of Brian's army-surplus coat.

"Anyone behind?" Dominick asked. Patiently Oran craned his neck to look out the rear window. Dominick slipped down in his seat, whistling shrilly between his teeth. The sound set Oran's nerves on edge. As the car lumbered towards the outskirts of the town, it was too small to contain the enormity of their anxiety.

Lar Morrison looked like he had been poured into a three-piece suit, and his neck lassoed by a bright fluorescent tie. His hair was brylcreamed into a shiny black helmet. Beneath it, his face was too small for the rest of his body; round and fresh-cheeked and made incongruous by a pair of eyebrows that wriggled like drunken caterpillars. They found him standing on the steps of a hotel in the main street with a gaggle of boys surrounded him. "Once you got a plan," Lar was saying, "there is nothing to it. Just put the plan into action..."

At that moment a man in a raincoat brushed past him to push open the door of the hotel. At the sight of him Lar was galvanised into action.

"Just a minute, newshound!" he said loudly, "I've a story for you."

Wistfully the man eyed the interior before he let go the door handle. "They won't print it," he said.

Lar ignored him and swung around to his audience which had been swollen by the three new arrivals. The reporter sighed. Reluctantly he dug a notebook out of his pocket and pulled out a biro. With a grandiloquent flourish, Lar lifted his arm to include everyone on the steps. "Let me introduce you. These young men here are members of the ALA," he said cheerfully. Dominick and Brian stiffened with surprise. Oblivious to the impact his words were making on them, Lar continued, "And I am their chief of staff. Tonight we're leading an assault on the courthouse. We'll have snipers covering the first unit of men. They'll be positioned there..." Lar waved towards the entrance to a laneway beside the hotel, "for a mopping-up operation." He dug his hands into his pockets and rocked back on his heels.

"What the fuck's he talking about? " Dominick

muttered.

But Lar was only getting into his stride. "Right?" he appealed to the crowd. Around him the boys shuffled. Lar was undaunted. "From now on it's war!" He jabbed his finger on to the reporter's note-pad. "Be sure to put that down."

"They won't print it," the reporter grimaced. "They never do." He sighed and thought of the bright lights of Dublin, of Fleet Street and the Pearl Bar. He slid past Lar and disappeared into the safety of the hotel. Already the boys had begun to drift away.

"So what can I do you for?" Cordially Lar turned his attention to Dominick.

Brian's mouth snapped shut. In a low voice Dominick said, "We need somewhere quiet to talk." Lar led them across the street and into the Ranchero bar. They went to the back of the pub and in to a snug. Lar poked his head around the door and then signalled the others to follow him inside. Once the pints were on the table Dominick came to the point. "We need a favour, Lar."

"Oh Jeez, lads!" Lar sat back comfortably in his seat. "I left you crowd—remember?" Glumly Dominick and Brian gazed into their glasses while Oran looked up at Lar with interest. "And wasn't I proved right in the end?" Lar asked rhetorically. "I said it would end up with British troops walking the streets. If you'd listened to me it would have been settled by now. I had it all worked out."

"You're right," Brian nodded amiably.

"Before your time, son." Lar turned conversationally to Oran. There was a pause. Lar smiled across the table at Dominick and Brian. "Of course, you're only a gang of sycophantic arse-lickers. No imagination, that's your trouble." He paused and swallowed a mouthful of beer. For a moment his eyes clouded.

Thoughtfully Dominick chased a mat across the table. Then his head reared up and he leant forward to look into Lar's face. "What's this ALA?" he asked. With relish Lar emphasised every syllable. "It's the Anti-Litter Army."

Another silence.

"Like it?" Lar wanted to know. A look of pain crossed Dominick's face. "For the Tidy Towns." Lar expanded on his theme. "It's a way of getting to the kids. You should see the bags of stuff we collect. I even have medals. They go mad for the medals. Discipline is a problem though. I had to courtmartial a young lad the other day. And he was one of the best in the unit."

A fly buzzed a requiem in the silence of the snug.

Suddenly Dominick snarled, " I suppose you knee-capped him!"

"Oh Jeez no!" Lar was shocked. "You'd never get the parents to stand for that."

Dominick stood up. His face was contorted with emotion. He jerked his head at Brian. The two men walked out of the snug. Lar opened his cavernous mouth and fed a whiskey into it and then a mouthful of stout. Delicately he wiped an edge of froth off his lips.

"So how's she cutting, son?" Lar directed his genial question at Oran. There didn't seem to be an answer to that one. Oran said nothing and ducked down over his glass. The silence deepened. Through the open door he could see Dominick and Brian still in whispered conversation. Brian nodded while Dominick spoke, agitatedly, into his ear.

After a while they returned. "We want you to hold something for us."

"Oh?"

"The Branch are giving us fierce trouble."

"Have ye it there?" Lar asked curiously.

"Yes." Dominick didn't move.

"Give it over. Here's as good a place as any." Lar showed no surprise when the revolver, wrapped in a plastic bag, slid across the table. As it disappeared into his jacket pocket, Lar leant confidentially against Oran's shoulder. "I tell you, son," he breathed into Oran's face, "once upon a time it was just Dominick and me. In the old days we trained those boys up in HQ when they were still wetting their pants. Remember, Dom? We had them out in the Wicklow mountains, training until they were ready to drop. Dominick was in the FCA then. He'd come up and give us the benefit of his training." Lar's eyes were dreamy with reminiscence. "Doesn't seem more than a few days ago."

Dominick smiled and drank deeply from his glass of stout. Oran had a picture of them ending up awash with drink and nostalgia and miles away from home but, to his surprise, Dominick stood up and drained his glass.

"What was his plan?" Oran asked curiously on the journey back to Galway. Brian sighed. Oran waited but all Brian said was that they couldn't afford to lose good men like Lar. The wipers whinged backwards and forwards across the windscreen, sweeping aside the sheets of rain.

"But what *was* his plan?" Oran persisted.

Brian straightened up. "Lar came up with a scheme. He worked in England for years on the buildings. The way things were over there, he said, you could kidnap the Queen and hold her for ransom. Her life in exchange for the Six Counties. He went to Buckingham Palace to check it all out. He said that the Brits were so stuck on her they would give us back the Six Counties just to secure her release. Lar knows his stuff. We passed the plan up to HQ but they wouldn't act on it. Lar went mad altogether when he heard that. He called for an inquiry into the army council. Then he wanted us to form a breakaway and do the job ourselves."

Silently Oran grappled with the notion of Dominick, Brian and Lar making off with the Queen of England. Brian paused and leant forward to peer into the rain-swept view ahead. "He said the army council was full of Brit-lovers." Brian spoke softly into the dark. "MacIntyre came down and gave him the works. Either shut up or get out. So he got out. Lar was a big loss, one of the best ever. The movement needs him. I wouldn't mind but that Dublin crowd wouldn't know a good plan if it got up and slapped them in the puss."

"Do you think it was a good plan? " Oran asked.

Brian pulled on his pipe. Any reply he might have made was prevented by a snort from the back seat.

"Him and his tidy towns!" Dominick was sparking with contempt. "Poncing around with do-gooders," he raged. "A member of the Republican movement. They've a lot to answer for up there in Dublin and MacIntyre along with them, in their pocket. Lar Morrison was a long-standing member before them jumped-up johnnies was ever heard of. In the old days an officer was treated with respect. Now he's a broken man. The Anti-Fucking-Litter-Army, for Jesus' sake!" For a moment Dominick was lost for words. When he spoke again his voice was virulent. "He could have gone to the top. Even been chief of staff one day but those bloody jackeens were out to break him."

After his outburst Dominick relapsed into gloomy silence. Brian's jowls settled into his collar as he peered into the dark. Nostalgia filled the car, a yearning for what might have been. As the car crept mournfully along the road, scraps of reminiscences floated up; stories of men on the run; friends dead and gone to England or fallen by the wayside on the road to Éire Nua. Oran understood then how tenuous was their survival; how shaky the foundation upon which the movement was built. When the world outside threatened, their only strength lay in bonds of loyalty, like a family holding together. He could not stand apart and judge them. One way or the other, they needed each other. It hurt him to hear the intimations of despair in Dominick's voice. Oran could think of nothing to say that would lighten the load. As he saw it, Brian and Dominick were the past, brittle and ailing, while he was the future, on the rise.

Two weeks later his opportunity came. When Dominick broke the news, Oran was ready to prove to himself and to the others, that the struggle would go on and that each generation replenishes the will to continue.

TWENTY-ONE

T he cottage where Brian lived looked sunken and empty. It was built at a lower level than the road and had a peaked roof and windows that strained worriedly through an overgrown garden hedge. A key dangled in the latch. Dominick didn't bother to knock and Oran and Kevin followed him in. The hall was dim and dusty and cold. Through a door came the sounds of a television and as they stepped into the bright kitchen a cozy domestic heat swirled up to greet them, redolent of boiled cabbage and turf-smoke and bacon fat.

When he saw them Brian stood up from his chair by the fire and shouted over the babble of the television. "Time to go to your bed, Mam." Her eyes intent on the glowing screen, the old woman ignored him. "Up...up," he insisted as if he were dealing with a recalcitrant child.

At last, hearing him, the old woman struggled out of the armchair and swayed across the room. When she reached the door she paused and turned. "I know what you're up to," she cackled unexpectedly, "so I do!"

They looked at her, amazed.

"Don't mind her," Brian dismissed her with a wave of his hand. "She's got so bad these days that she only knows it's Sunday when the priest calls to tell her."

While the old woman rumbled through the house the four members of the active service unit sat down to watch the end of the quiz programme. At last, the credits rolled up and Brian leant forward to switch off the television. "Your man from Mullingar was an eejit," said Kevin, "never getting past the sixpenny questions." No-one said anything.

With uncharacteristic deliberation Dominick cleared a space on the mantelpiece. He leant his elbow among the bric-à-brac and rested his chin on his hand.

"Pay attention, men." The others looked at him. The silence was broken only by the sound of the fire crackling in the grate. He said quietly, "MacIntyre's given us the go-ahead."

A bubbling sigh escaped from the pipe clenched between Brian's lips. A coal tumbled onto the hearth and idly, Dominick bent down and chased it into the grate with his foot. "Any word of this gets out and we're all done for." He stopped for a moment to chew frantically on his knuckle. Oran leant forward to hear what he would say next.

"It's a big one. We're going to do Heaney's place." Excitement coursed around the room. Oran sat back and grinned. Heaney's factory! He couldn't have made a better choice himself. Fergus was going to get his way after all and who deserved it more? "We're going to clean it out," Dominick continued, "There's good stuff there. We need a truck. Lar's the man for that. And both of you," he pointed at Oran and Kevin, "will get inside the building and bring the stuff out. Brian and me will be in the lane with the truck. Once we've loaded up we'll drive it to a transfer point. MacIntyre takes it from there. And meanwhile," he paused and directed his attention at Oran and Kevin, "you two will set fire to the factory."

Set fire to it! Oran was astonished. Enough to forget himself and without thinking, he did the unthinkable. He challenged Dominick. "What do you want to do that for?" he asked.

"Orders, Reidy. If you're able to take them, that is." Dominick's voice bristled with anger.

"No, of course I am," Oran was contrite. He felt his face stiffen with embarrassment. "I just wondered," he mumbled. "Sorry." And then he saw Dominick's eyelid droop. In the next moment Dominick turned away and continued to address the others. But as he listened, Oran wondered at the turn that events had taken and tried to ferret out the logic behind Dominick's wink.

Suddenly it dawned on him. This was to be a gesture of solidarity with the men on strike. Their criticism of Fergus had been nothing more than a smoke-screen, a security precaution while, on the quiet, Dominick and Brian had been setting things up. All the time they had been waiting for the go-ahead from MacIntyre. The pieces were falling into place. Laughable how stupid he had been not to see it before. He sat up straight and paid attention and kept his mouth tight shut. This is important...the message drummed in his head as the plan of action unfolded. The palms of his hands were clammy with sweat and, surging along his skin, there was a new sensation like high-tensile energy.

"*I've made it!*" he wanted to shout. "*Do you hear me, mother, I've made it!*"

TWENTY-TWO

As the days passed by Oran slipped into a rhythm. He sawed planks and hammered in nails and cleared away the old wood. Secretly he was preparing himself for the real work ahead. There was an inevitability, a rightness about it that enabled him to face the future calmly. Soothed by the regularity of his days, his mind was free to wander without fear and he could only hope when the moment came, his serenity would not desert him. Time passed in daily repetitious tasks. At night he slept without dreaming.

In the attic room, motes of dust hovered along the shafts of morning light. The studio looked larger and brighter than it had before. All the partitions had been cleared away and where the old floor had been taken up, the new boards gleamed whitely.

Deep in thought, Jane sat in the middle of the room, her chin resting on her hands, and sighed. "I wonder what I should put there?" She stood up and pointed to a large alcove in the gable wall. Oran looked blank. More money than sense, he decided and kept his mouth shut. He had become accustomed to Jane O'Molloy and the way she had of drifting in and out of the studio. These days, most of the time, she left him alone to enjoy the quiet monotony of the work. It reminded him of working for his father on good days, the lifting and carrying, out of the cool dim space and into the sunshine of the yard.

Jane lost interest in the alcove. "There's an auction in Roundstone. The notice in the paper has a list of building stuff that's coming up. You can tell me what's worth buying. Meet me in the yard at eleven." Crisp and authoritative, her voice brooked no argument. Oran bent down over his work. Bitch, he thought, his day spoiled.

Outside the sun struggled through a morning haze. Very deliberately, he washed his hands under the tap while she waited. As he wiped his hands she gave a snort of impatience.

"We don't have all day," she said shortly, ignoring his ghost of a smile.

They walked towards the gate in the wall that surrounded the stableyard. There was a sudden awkward moment as their fingers collided. Who should go first, employer or employee? Should he open the door or should he leave it to her? The battle of fingers for the long sleek bolt...I've done this before, Oran thought. Puzzled he stood stock still, his eyes narrowing against the light as he trawled in his memory. Then he saw her amused expression and reddening, he stepped back and allowed her open the door.

At that moment it came to him…his first memory; of winter sunlight, a brightness seeping through a curtain of mist as he stood in the yawning aperture of the kitchen doorway. Under his fingernails, the door-jamb, brittle with flaking paint that he picked at, loosening dark-green flecks with their astonishingly white undersides. A mixture of smells; the sick sweetness issuing from the abattoir nearby, smoke dying out of chimneys and fresh hay bundled outside the shed in the yard. Underlying the comfortable smells, there was another; a stench of horse-dung, telling shame-filled secrets of dirtied trousers in the playground, the private calvaries of childhood that are revived in the sight of an animal lifting its tail to ease out fat rolls of excrement.

A yard stretched out, long and narrow, a series of sheds at the far end, a stable-door hanging off its hinges, revealing straw-coloured gloom. Further off, beyond the lichened walls, there were massed roofs, chimney-stacks, dormers, the gables of brick and stone, and slates slipping on to crumbling parapets— the chaotic construction of a Dublin roofscape. Two great doors spanned by a zig-zag of timber bracing were the focus of his childish concern. Closed and bolted, their heavy bolt-pins lying snug and greasy in their cases, the flaphandle dangling down. As their acolyte, Oran attended upon them. He waited for them to shiver and for the panels of the doors to become alive, thundering under the call to "Open up!" as he ran to unloose the stays that imprisoned a monster capable of rattling the doors into a cacophony; and had the power to prise his mother out of the kitchen, grumbling, "wait a minute, can't you, wait a minute," as she battled with Oran for possession of the long bolts sliding back on their cradles, releasing, as they went, the two archangel wings that opened out to frame a triumphant arrival.

First came the cavernous face that was almost human, huge in scale, a long-nosed, heavy-eyed face, with soft mouth chewing on the bit. The mare's bones collared in leather and brasses that clinked when she swung her head impatiently. Beyond the muscular greatness of her flanks rose up a man's face, satanically black. The only discernible features were his eyes, white fragments adrift on a dark sea. A sack, weighty with coal-dust, flowed about his shoulders. On the expanse of the dray, its partners lay shrunken and wasted. This was his father; possessor of unbelievable powers, who could lift him up with one arm and carry Oran through dangerous air to place him on the plateau beside him.

"Give me!" shouted Oran, intoxicated by his ascent and the unsteady rhythm of the dray, the clop-clop of hooves on cobbles and the rough thong threaded between his fingers. As he crouched in the cavern made by his father's body he became part of the creaking, swaying, jingling, glorious pageant.

In the car Jane O'Molloy was silent. And in a hurry. She drove so fast that Oran caught only a glimpse of a familiar blue Cortina parked at a bus-stop. He turned away. Once they were well on the way to Roundstone he chanced a look in the mirror and his heart plummeted. What class of a gobdaw was Moran, anyhow, to be following him out into bogland? Oran shook his head involuntarily, as if trying to shake off the car with its two occupants. For a while the small intrusion in the rear mirror persisted and then, as inexplicably as it had appeared, the car vanished out of view.

Oran took a deep breath. In the distance, bunches of seaweed glistened along the margins of the rocky coast. A series of promontories, each distinct in the limpid Connemara light, nudged a way into deep water. Along their ridges, black and white cattle grazed in the grass. And further out towards the horizon, islands, blue and hump-backed like whales, broke the surface of the sea. These were pastoral images from Bord Fáilte promotions. Even up close, the countryside looked unreal; the colours too gorgeous, the contrasts too extreme. He would have preferred to stay in the dusty atmosphere of the studio, instead of travelling out in this exposed country with this woman. She made him feel uncomfortable although her conversation was harmless enough. Above the chit-chat, her eyes displayed an unexplained curiosity and her glance travelled over him with an intensity that he found unnerving.

In the village of Roundstone the church hall was deserted. The doors leading into the hall were locked and a poster fluttered in the breeze. Jane and Oran climbed slowly out of the car as a silence hollowed out the air around them.

"Shit!" she said loudly. Her anger profaned the wide bleak expanse of tarmac. "The bloody auction isn't until two o'clock. In Galway they told me it was on at twelve. Isn't that just typical?"

Oran spread his fingers out on the bonnet of the car and said nothing. He was stiff after the drive and every bump on the road had been imprinted on his arse. Typical of what?

Jane got back into the car and sat for a moment, frowning at the closed doors before revving up the engine. Oran smiled. The world, he was learning, had been designed, as far as people like Jane O'Molloy were concerned, to serve them. It was difficult for her to conceive of it being otherwise. He took his time about getting back into the car. Once he was in the passenger seat beside her, she swung the car violently around on the carpark. She was still seething when she turned the car off the main road and on to a narrow track leading down towards the sea.

On the crest of a sand-dune, the car bumped to a standstill. Ahead of them the sea sweltered in a noon-day summer heat. Jane got out and stretched her arms above her head.

"Shit!" she yelled, "Shitshitshitshit!" Indignantly, in response, a crowd of seagulls leapt into the sky. "That's better." She smiled at Oran, "Fancy a drink?" Without waiting for an answer she leant into the car and withdrew a bottle of whiskey out of the glove compartment. She unscrewed the top and took a mouthful. Then she handed the bottle to Oran.

The dunes fell steeply down onto a deserted beach. On either side, the beach curved away in an arc of white sand.

"Tell me," she said, looking straight at him. From her, it was as much an order as a request. "Why were those men following us?"

Oran felt like one of the seagulls that she had scattered so casually with her shouts.

"I didn't see anyone," he mumbled.

She laughed. "You're an awful liar."

"Were there men behind us?"

"Don't you know there were. Weren't you sitting on the edge of your backside, and watching with one eye on the road and the other on them? I don't know which you were more afraid of, my driving or those men."

He grimaced and, without comment, followed her along the beach. Sand flooded their shoes and she bent down to slip off her sandals.

"I'll have to guess if you don't tell me. You're an international jewel thief. You're a drug dealer. Interpol are after you." She smiled mischievously. "You slept with that man's wife." Oran laughed shortly. "No, not that? Well then, a gambling debt? Your landlady looking for her rent?" She began to giggle. "I won't stop until you tell me."

He answered her slowly, and not without a certain sense of his own importance. "It's political."

"Aaah!" she responded knowingly. "One of Dominick's boys."

They fell silent. In the distance waves rose and sank with a measured shushashusha, curling into foam and then sliding out along the beach.

"So you're planning to free Ireland?" she asked.

"I'm going to try," he replied solemnly, aware that she was still making fun of him.

As long as I pretend, she thought, that we actually belong to different countries we can probably communicate quite well. We can lie back on the sand and discuss life and philosophy and the universe. It's a question of tolerance. Or indifference. You're a terrorist, how fascinating! Do tell me about yourself.

"Do you really believe in all that stuff?" It sounded more arrogant that she had intended. Oh, pardon me, my opinions are showing. What the hell, she spent too much of her life apologising. She felt a sudden empathy with Carol and her inclination to tilt at windmills. Even if her actions were blind and self-destructive they were a sign of independence. Or was it a matter of cause and effect, a mindless response that would wither if the stimulus were withdrawn?

"You might be better employed getting us back into the Commonwealth." she said.

"Never!" Oran replied hotly. "We're an independent people. We should be proud of that." He straightened up, ready to argue.

"It all depends what you mean by independent. Look at Galway! If it weren't for the multinationals we'd all starve."

And if she weren't paying his wages, he would have laughed into her face, and her eyes squinting at him across the sand.

"You probably think that people will always be kept down on their knees," he said. "But there comes a time when every man has to decide where he stands."

"In the North?"

"Yes," he hesitated. "There, more than anywhere." She cocked her head and waited for him to elaborate, enjoying the argument for its own sake. Frustrated by his own inarticulacy, Oran strode down to the water's edge. The inadequacy of his words reflected a confusion inside him of which he was all too aware. Suddenly he had a vision of Fergus, shedding a past that no longer had any meaning for him and reaching out to an unknown future. Even Fergus wanted the foreigners in. Sinn Féin meant Mé Féin, he said, while foreign companies brought jobs and the organisation of workers.

Jane took another mouthful of whiskey and

watched Oran come to a halt on the wet sand. She wanted to follow him and argue, to pull him up short and give him a piece of her mind. Then her irritation dissipated as a new idea bubbled up to take its place. I'll show you, young man, she grinned to herself, that there's more to life than border politics. Oran sensed her presence at his shoulder as her hand brushed his sleeve. Suspicious that she might continue her baiting, he ignored her.

"Isn't that a magnificent day?" she said instead. It was. The mountains rose skywards, every knuckled slope etched out in the sunshine. Brushstrokes of cloud were daubed across the sky. "Would you dare a swim?" Her eyes were taunting him as she pointed towards the water. "Would you?"

Puzzled, he looked to where she pointed. It was warm enough and his legs still ached from the drive. Why not?

"But I haven't any..." he stopped, blocked by suspicion. He was not prepared for the sight of her bending down there, in front of him. Despite the heat of the sun he felt a shivering in his skin as her body started to unfold out of her clothes. Hypnotised, he watched as she rolled up her shirt and under-clothes. He had no other thought except of the globes of her breasts and the dark cleft between her legs. He was mute, overpowered by the urgency to be naked alongside her, to pull her down under him on to the warm sand, her legs opening and her mouth sweetly receiving his tongue. She looked sideways at him, and saw it too, the double-backed beast in his eyes. She smiled and then turned away to bound triumphantly down the beach. When the water hit her skin she shrieked with delight.

Rapidly Oran moved down the beach and once he was at a safe distance, waited for her to come out of the water. Digging furiously with the toe of his shoe into the sand he stood, face burning, when she emerged out of the water and rubbed herself dry with her shirt. Even so, he could sense her amusement rippling like the waves of the sea, across the sand to touch him. He couldn't tell that she wasn't laughing at him. Nor that the only focus of her amusement was herself.

Why on earth did she do it, Jane wondered. It's like a kid showing off. Prick-teasing for the sake of it. If he weren't so innocent he would realise that he could have her now, here, on the sand, just as he desired. She smiled tenderly at the back of his neck. I'm not just cheap, young man, she mouthed at him, I'm free. She dawdled over her dressing and wondered what he looked like inside his clothes. Eventually she was dressed and she walked across the sand to where he faced out to sea.

"Like some?" She presented the whiskey to him like a peace offering. He glowered at her and took a mouthful.

"That's better." Again she cocked her head to one

side and looked at him quizzically. "I suppose you do realise that Dominick is a lunatic." Unconsciously she was echoing Matt Moran's sentiments. Oran shrugged and took another gulp of whiskey. Why should he take any risks arguing with her? It was a dangerous subject. With the job coming up, there was too much at stake to be taking chances. Better to shift the conversation away from himself. He turned and handed her back the bottle. Then, for the first time, he looked at her full in the face.

"So what do you believe in?" he said tightly. And was satisfied to see her eyes widen in shock. His challenge hung, quivering and unanswered in the air. From far out to sea came the wail of herring -gulls and the thin plaint of a flock of oyster-catchers. A fish lifted itself out of the water and plopped back in again. Around them, the silence shifted and settled into an almost companionable intimacy. Without answering Oran's question, she lifted the bottle, and saluted him before she put the whiskey to her lips.

"Touché..." Jane said silently .

"Oh, Jane!"

Mama's face was huge, bleak, accusatory. Hers was a voice trammelled by a lifetime of inhibition. Dada was in there too, somewhere, rummaging around in the background. Guilt nibbling at her, Jane turned her back on the pair of them and faced the door. Resolutely, she twisted the knob. Once she was certain

that the door would open to release her, she made up
her mind to have the last word.

"It's my life," she said, "I can do what I want." But
it was an ovine bleat, capable of convincing no-one.
Least of all, herself. She pushed the door open. In the
sitting-room, a chorus of voices rushed up to greet
her. Carol was sitting on the sofa, surrounded by
people, old schoolfriends, neighbours, women of her
own age. Madge Heaney teetered on the arm of the
sofa, giggling foolishly. Carol had them all in stitches.

"On the beach," Carol rocked back in amusement,
displaying her fillings. "Stark naked, the pair of them.
His little bum going up and down, up and down."

"Oh Carol!" Jane wailed, unconscious that she was
mirroring Mama's censure. Carol looked up and saw
her. Tears of laughter sparkled in her eyes.

"The Special Branch have it all over town," Carol
said, "and you expect me to keep quiet about it?" She
bounced on the sofa, consumed with merriment. "Up
and down, up and down."

Jane shuddered. A voice in her ear was shouting,
making unintelligible demands. I didn't do anything,
Jane tried to exonerate herself. It wasn't me...

The voice of authority was squeaky. Up through
banks of sleep Jane emerged. She muttered at the
pain of her shoulder and then daylight sluiced
between her eyelids. It was a dream, a dream. After
the realisation the guilt returned, muted to a grumble.
Up and down, up and down...Jane grimaced. Not

caught yet.

Beside her bed, the litte boy stood back and stared at her furiously. "You're late for school, Mum. It's half past eight and I want my breakfast." His eyes were big and trusting, the flecks of hazel reflecting those in her own. She swung her legs out of the bed and put on her dressing-gown and then chivvied the child out of her bedroom and down the corridor towards the kitchen.

Debris of a hasty breakfast littered the kitchen table. A cereal packet lay on its side, its contents strewn out among the dirty plates. Bits of burnt toast, a spoon sticky with marmalade, spilt sugar, cold teabags abandoned on the draining-board. In the mirror she could see that sleep had puffed up her eyes and flattened her hair. God, she thought, I mustn't let him see me like this. And then. Why not, for Christ sake? He's only the hired hand. Self-loathing filled her throat like a sour taste but, even while she argued with herself, she was slapping cold water on her face, fluffing out her hair, selecting what clothes to wear. Not the denim shirt, she decided, too severe for a woman her age. What does it matter? The child was munching his way through his bowl of cornflakes. In his hair, there were bits of food lodged among the tangles. She ran a hairbrush through it quickly until he whimpered from the pain. Hurry, hurry, or we'll be late.

Finally, he was ready, more or less. His hair only

rumpled, his shorts only slightly stained. I'm always settling for too little, she accused herself, for second-best; grubby clothes and unwashed hair for my children, and flirting with the hired hand for me. Why couldn't she be a proper wife and mother? Instead of having this obsession. The child heading out late for school because his mother had men on the brain. Get me out of this, someone. She prayed into the silence as if there were someone there to pray to. But there wasn't, she reminded herself, and even if there were, He would be a man. She sank her head in expiation on to the shoulder of the little boy and put her arms around him.

The boy struggled to be free. "Come on, Mum!" he urged her, "we'll be late."

Head down, she drove through the traffic, thinking of Garret. She needed to be close to him, to smell his skin, to feel his hands on her face. This was a frenzy that only he could ease.

"Mum!" In his agitation the little boy jumped about in the back seat. "You're going past the school."

She cursed and slowed the car down to a stop. The little boy got out and turned to kiss her. When she closed her eyes momentarily, and felt the warmth of his nose nuzzling against her cheek, it was as if it were the touch of a man.

Slowly she made her way home, the prospect of the vacant rooms ready to swallow her up. Where else could she go? There was no Carol to lean on now. A wave of self-pity engulfed Jane. It was only ten o'clock in the morning and already, she was drifting.

Then she saw them walking along the pavement. Two figures she would have recognised anywhere; Ken, her brother-in-law, tall and lanky, accompanied by his oldest daughter Caroline. There was something consoling about the way the plump twelve-year-old girl waddled past, carrying a shopping-bag on her arm. Carol's way of walking. That child, thought Jane, ought to be at school. She rolled down the car window.

"Ken!" she called, "how are you?" What did one say in the circumstances? It wasn't a funeral after all so commiserations weren't in order. Uncertain as to how Ken would react Jane had decided to wait a decent interval before calling to the house. Now chance was providing her with an unexpected opportunity. "Would you like a lift?"

"No, thanks," Ken answered her quickly, his face expressionless. Keep away, his tone of voice said.

There was a terrifying self-sufficiency about the two of them, father and daughter, as they stood alongside the car, the shopping-bag dangling like booty between them. "Caroline is just going to do the shopping," he continued.

"Need any help?" The words sounded officious but they were out before Jane could stop herself.

"Oh no, we're doing just fine, aren't we?" Ken deferred to the girl, his eyes solemn behind his glasses.

"Caroline is a great manager."

The girl pushed her shoulders back and looked up proudly at her father. Her little housewife look got on Jane's nerves. Caroline is not a manager, she wanted to argue, she's a little girl who ought to be at school. Instead she changed the subject and asked, "Have your heard from Carol?" It was wiser, she decided, not to mention the postcard that had arrived a few days after Carol's departure and the cryptic message scrawled over it. *Rejoice! I have learnt a language and know how to curse in it...*Standing in the hallway, the rest of the letters bundled in her hands, Jane had pored over those words. She had barely an inkling of what they meant, but she had smiled all the same, reassured by their bravado.

Ken shook his head.

"Oh, you know Carol." Jane was anxious to comfort them both. "She always has some crazy scheme hatching."

Ken and Caroline did not reply. They made such an incongruous couple, Jane thought with a pang, so out of place among the morning shoppers heading down to buy groceries. A lanky threadbare owl of a man and a fat little girl among so many women. Ken and Caroline gazed at her, each with the same woebegone expression in their eyes.

"Are you sure I can't help?"

"We can do the shopping very well," Ken said stiffly. Without blinking, Caroline stared ahead and clutched the shopping-bag to her hip. Beneath her fringe, the little girl's forehead was furrowed.

"It's all a bit of nonsense," Jane continued hurriedly. "I'm sure in a week or so, Carol will get tired of Dublin and she'll come back home." Jane wanted to convince them that what she was saying was true; that Carol's departure was nothing more than a silly prank. But she was conscious that, no matter what she wanted them to believe, or wanted to believe herself, life rolled on relentlessly. Ken looked different, less helpless than he usually did. Managing...that was what he was doing.

"Come back home?" he echoed in surprise.

"Of course she will," Jane said reassuringly.

His face was closed up like a cul-de-sac. When he spoke there wasn't a hint of a tremor in his dry, colourless voice. "That bitch," he said, "had better not try."

TWENTY-THREE

"**K**en was so definite about it," said Jane sadly. "I've never seen him so definite about anything before. He'll never take her back after this."

Across the dinner-table Richard shrugged. "That marriage was doomed from the start," he said.

Doomed. Again the old image of her sister materialised. Carol had only gone as far as Dublin, Jane reassured herself and, knowing Carol, the whole business could still be nothing more than a bit of nonsense. But the joyful phrase rang in her head. *I've learnt a new language...*

Jane pushed away her empty plate. Richard gave her a sidelong glance and said, "I promised I'd call over to my mother this evening." Jane did not respond. "She'd like to see you, Jane, you know how much she enjoys your visits." Jane set her mouth in a stubborn line of resistance. "I just thought you might like to come with us. The whole family. We could all go over and give her a surprise."

"I'm busy tonight," Jane said bad-temperedly. Her words lingered on to accuse her. She changed tack. "I'm with the kids all day," she pleaded. "Give me a break."

Richard smiled his wide lazy smile and picked up the newspaper. "For you, dear," he drawled, "I'd do anything."

As she got the children ready to go with Richard she felt a start of fear. What was she doing? This double life could undermine her very existence. Did undermine it. While the children struggled to get their shoes on, she ran her fingers along the balustrade of the staircase and wondered how it was that all the familiar things that she had ever touched were threatened, contaminated by it. You will go, Monique, because I say so! The au pair shadowed her up the hall as Jane opened the front door to let the children out. Outside, the air was heavy with the smell of newly-cut grass. An evening sun cast long shadows across the lawn and the children's nylon jackets glowed an iridescent blue. Heady with excitement they skittered like puppies around on the gravel.

Happiness is so precarious, she thought, always running towards extinction. She would have liked to have held, to have preserved in some way, the contrast their blondness made with the kingfisher clothes they wore, and the way their hair framed their young faces like the yellow hoods of flowers.

"Will you be back?" she muttered, her face sunk momentarily into Richard's collar, wanting to gather up for safe-keeping all the elusive strands of husband and children that drifted around her like weed in a current. Conscious of how close she was to betrayal, she was relieved when he misheard her.

"Around nine o'clock, I suppose. I'll put the kids to bed. You take your time coming home. Are you going to see Madge?"

Her face pink, Jane nodded. What a lousy liar I am, she thought. I can't even manage to be a good conspirator.

TWENTY-FOUR

In the laneway Dominick leant out of the window of the truck. His eyes were craters in his bony face. Drops of sweat glistened on his forehead.

"Make sure you're not seen by anyone round at the front."

"OK."

"Remember, take out all the stuff first."

"Yeah."

"And, for Jesus sake, don't forget. Keep out of sight of the caravan."

"Yeah, OK."

It was impossible to disguise Kevin. Even with a balaclava pulled down over his face, his height was a betrayal.

The lock of the factory gates broke apart in Oran's hands.

"Jeez!" breathed Kevin, "some people ask to be robbed."

Oran led the way into the factory yard. Close to his shoulder, Kevin followed him in. The two boys edged around the corner of the building in search of the broken window that Dominick had pinpointed for them. As they crept forward, the darkness solidified comfortingly around them. The window was broken all right; a bit of paper was taped over it to keep out the draughts. Delicately Kevin dipped his arm inside and opened the casement.

Inside, the building was intimidatingly high, with the formality of a church. Long aisles formed by stacks of packing-cases stretched down its length. As they picked their way along one of the aisles, Oran felt his skin pulsate, not with fear but with exhilaration at the ease of it all. He was enjoying himself and he laughed in the dark.

"What's so funny?" Kevin wanted to know, his voice quavering.

"Nothing. Give me a hand."

"Another one?" Kevin giggled foolishly. "And you with two of your own."

His laughter bordered on hysteria.

"Sssh!" Oran stood stock still. "Listen!" he mouthed at Kevin as he sensed some discreet undefined movement among the packing-cases. A mouse, perhaps, or a rat? The balaclava hid Kevin's face. He kept his mouth clamped shut but his eyes shifted all over the place. Suddenly he hiccuped loudly.

"Shut up!" Oran hissed.

A silence welled up around them. Somewhere a distant train howled. Whoooooo. And then nothing. Cautiously Oran began to move forward again, Kevin clutching his arm. He took note of his surroundings. On either side there were boxed typewriters stacked neatly in cases. Just waiting to be taken. There was more stuff here than they could manage. Once they got the doors open Lar's truck would be filled up in no time. Two journeys maybe. And he grinned again in the dark. MacIntyre would be impressed by that.

He kept moving down the aisle while, around him, the gloom intensified. He could have been gliding on ice for all the sound he made and, at his shoulder, Kevin too was moving quietly, his breath rhythmic and easy. There was nothing to it. In and out in a jiffy like the bishop said to the actress. A laugh rumbled in his gut. He was the one in control now. He'd show them how it was done.

Then they both heard it. The sound. Clear and irrefutible.

"O mother!"

It was coming towards them.

"What is it?"

Along his collar, hairs stiffened. Beside him Kevin panted like a dog. What was it? On his skin the balaclava was hot now, unbearable.

"What is it? What is it"

For a moment, nothing and then:

"No!"

A scream pumped out of him at the sudden brilliance bursting on his eyeballs. The light up ahead was swinging wide, and next, right up close, in front of them both.

"Hit it, hit it, hit it," Oran yelled, panic pouring through him like water. Kevin lifted something out of his pocket, something heavy that exploded in that high space, reverberating around their ears in a loud staccato boom.

The light skewed out of control and smashed on to the concrete.

"Jesus!" Kevin whimpered. "Oh, Jesus, Mary and Joseph. Oh, Jesus!"

They had both seen it, in the split-second between the explosion and the light going out. They had seen the face; an ancient, grandfatherly face, frozen, for an instant, with shock and then no longer anything recognisable as it disintegrated into a sponge of bloody flesh.

Kevin moaned and the sour faecal smell of his fear filled Oran's nostrils.

"Oh, Mammy!" The schoolboy dropped the gun and twisted away from Oran. He ran wildly down along the aisle of packing-cases, his boots clattering a harsh diminuendo along the concrete floor.

Lying face downwards, the night-watchman could have been mistaken for a bundle of clothing in the dark. Except for the blood seeping between the strands of hair at his neck and the warmth of his skin when Oran, without thinking, bent to touch his head. He stretched out his hand as if seeking reassurance but what he touched was soft pulp and shattered bone that gave way in his fingers. At that moment he wanted to run like Kevin, run out of the place and keep running. Away from them all; Dominick, Brian, Kevin, all of them who were reduced to nothing, when set against the horror filling his stomach. Most of all, he wanted to run away from this thing, spread-eagled on the ground at his feet.

Spread out; get rid of the gun.

Dumbly, he listened to the orders, distinct inside his head. This and then the next thing. He was no fool. The gun was evidence, he continued to advise himself as he moved like someone pushing through mud at an achingly slow pace, brushing his hand in wide arcs across the floor, careful not to touch the body again, searching for one thing only.

"Where is it? Where is it?"

The question hammered inside his brain until he felt his eyes water. Christ damn it. To cry now. He could feel a smarting sensation along the inside of his eye-lids. He coughed, trying to clear the strange acrid taste out of his throat but it only made it harder to breathe. Behind him somewhere, he heard an explosion of windows shattering. Then a tide of smoke engulfed him.

"Dominick!" he wanted to shout, "are you trying to kill me?"

He crouched down near the ground and then at last, found what he was looking for. Cold and hard at his fingertips. He grasped the gun. It felt substantial, almost comforting. At last he could face the flames tearing up along the aisle. Bent low he ran towards the exploded window, feeling the heat of the flames scorch along his side.

Weeping and laughing, he collapsed to his knees on the tarmac outside and swallowed great gulps of air.

"Holy Mother!" he wept, ripping the balaclava off his throbbing skin.

His way back was cut off by thick black smoke and flames shooting up the side of the building. Ahead he knew, or at least he hoped, lay the way through to the front gates. To safety. Blindly, he groped his way along the narrow passage between the perimeter wall and the factory. He was totally alone, and tumbling forward into a smoke-filled darkness. Black fire, he thought confusedly, hell and damnation. His ribs hurt from the exertion of keeping ahead of it. He would suffocate and die, he knew it. The passage-way was narrow and he was terrified that further up ahead he would find it blocked. The idea dogged him as he stumbled along the passageway, without knowing whether it offered a chance of escape or led him towards a dead-end .

So engrossed was he that the men were close up to him before he realised that there was anyone else in the passage. In his confusion he thought for a moment that Dominick and the others were appearing out of the smoke. The men had their coats off and were using them to beat down the flames. Although the fire was burning fiercely through the building, their determination didn't let up. Near to Oran a thin wiry figure was contorted with the effort of pulling a blanket around. The next moment, the figure swung around and, with a manic force, drove the blanket against the flames. His face came out of the darkness, white and wet with sweat.

It was Fergus. But a changed Fergus. One who was suddenly immense and roaring unintelligibly. When he turned towards Oran, recognition flooded his eyes.

"You stupid bastard!"

He dropped the blanket and Oran found himself being grabbed and rammed up hard against the wall. A searing pain came from somewhere inside his skin.

Enraged, he struggled to break free but the grip Fergus had on him was like a vice.

"Jesus, it's what you wanted," Oran's voice was a hoarse croak above the crackling of the fire.

"Wanted?" Fergus thrust his fist against Oran's throat. The boy's eyes were deep murderous holes in which fires died without trace.

"You've gone and burnt down our factory," Fergus yelled and Oran felt his legs weaken. Then unexpectedly, Fergus let go and fell back against the wall alongside him. A sob wracked in his throat as he threw his head back against the granite.

"Oh my God," he groaned. "Heaney's won after all."

Oran stood, hypnotised by the words that made no sense.

"Our labour built this factory," Fergus continued, almost dreamily. "First we had the factory and then we had the town. The whole town was with us. The whole fucking country was with us and still the bastard has won." He groaned and rolled away from Oran to face the wall. "He even gets the insurance. What a joke..."

"But you said about a bomb!" Oran shouted into his ear.

"What?" Fergus lifted his face and gazed at Oran in astonishment.

Oran nodded. "Don't you remember you said it to Dominick? And so I told them about the strike and how you needed support."

"Dominick put you up to it," Fergus said flatly, "for the Cause. Christ, the innocence! Don't you even know what you've done?"

Oran couldn't breathe. His throat was closed like a knot.

"So Dominick told you to burn the factory?"

"Yes."

"And who told Dominick?"

It was only then that Oran understood. Sobbing, he stumbled along the passageway, his knuckles up to his eyes to protect himself against the heat, but the flames that scorched him now came from somewhere inside his head.

Out of the darkness a fireman, massive in his oilskins, loomed up in front of Oran and grabbed his arm. Beyond the fireman's shoulder Oran was able to make out the outline of the front gates and the crowds of people who were milling around a fire-tender straddling the entrance. Behind him, timbers fell in a burst of angry flames.

"Are there any more in there?"

Oran nodded. The fireman plunged down the passage. Another one rose up to take his place immediately and grabbed Oran. Too weak to resist, Oran succumbed and was propelled the last few steps until he reached the entrance. Within minutes, the crowd had encompassed him. Dazed he looked around. So many people...where did they all come from? He focused on a lone figure who was prancing around inside the gates.

"Yeeeeee-haaaw!"

It was Donie Conneally.

The student was waving his arms in the air and whooping like a drunken cowboy. At the sight of him Oran felt a sense of relief. At least, here was someone who was familiar without being dangerous.

"Let's burn the city down and start again," Donie was hollering at the top of his voice. Grateful for the diversion, Oran managed a stiff smile. Smiling, he discovered, made his face ache. His eyes still smarted and his eyelashes seemed to have disappeared in the fire. Jesus, he wondered, was that some kind of evidence? People were coming in on all sides, drawn by the spectacle, and the scale of destruction. With a crash, another roof-timber collapsed and Oran's ears filled with whistles and shouts. He ignored the crowd and concentrated instead on Donie's yeeeeee-haaaw yells.

"Get back!" a fireman roared, forcing the crowd into a temporary retreat beyond the gates. In the crush, Oran lost sight of Donie.

Then he remembered the gun .

It dragged in his coat-pocket like a bad conscience. His whole body shook, the pain from the fire dying down to be replaced by a cold wet terror slapping up inside his stomach. Get rid of the gun. He instructed his legs to walk, not too fast or he would attract attention, and not too slow.

"Just so," he muttered, "that's very good."

At the bridge over the Corrib he leant over the parapet and dropped the gun into the water. They couldn't afford to lose a firearm but they'd been stupid enough to trust Kevin with it in the first place. And an old man dead. Don't think about it. Nerves of steel, Dominick's voice spoke inside him, that's what you need in this business.

Head of steel was more like it.

Calm down.

Act normally.

Oran looked down into the river as it eased its bulk between the arches of the bridge. In the dark sky sparks flickered upward. A breeze fanned across his face, damping down the ache in his eyes and slowly his breath eased. He ran his fingers through his hair.

"Take your time," Oran counselled Oran. He remained where he was, leaning on the parapet. It was like a dream. Real and unreal. Take stock. Where are you now? Where are you going? Christ! he panicked, where *could* he go? He would take his time. There was no reason why someone like him wouldn't be leaning against the stone parapet of the Corrib bridge and watching the most talked about factory in Galway as it went up in flames. Just as long as he acted normally.

"Now there's a fire to warm the cockles of a TD's heart!" Close to his ear a voice smashed through his defences. With sinking heart Oran turned to acknowledge the figure standing beside him.

A fire to warm the cockles...His face glowing, Donie Conneally leant against the parapet and peered into Oran's face.

"You got a bit of a roasting," he said. His expression had a knowingness that frightened Oran. He steeled himself but Donie's mercurial attention had already shifted.

"Heard the news?"

"What news?" Oran asked thickly.

"There's a hooley in O'Shea's tonight."

Companionably Donie took Oran's arm. Again, Oran felt the cognitive spark.

He knows, Oran thought but, too weak to resist, he began to accompany Donie across the bridge towards the centre of the town.

"Old man O'Shea has finally got someone to take Molly off his hands," Donie continued. Molly O'Shea was a big coarse girl who worked behind the bar and was known as the Ride of Woodquay. "A lad from Athenry, God help us," Donie said piously. "Still the pub'll come to him in time when he finds he cannot support her in the manner to which she is accustomed."

His dirty laugh was so close that Oran could smell the beer sickening on his breath. Sometimes it is enough just to be alive, to feel the tide of the world running like the swollen river beneath your feet.

"There'll be no closing tonight," said Donie. "Are you coming?"

It was some kind of alibi, the only one he would be likely to muster in the circumstances. Weighing up the options he didn't have much choice. Clumsily Oran stood to attention and gave Donie his best Óglaigh na hÉireann salute that he'd been practising.

"Lead the way, chief," he said.

But the hand that brushed his forehead came bearing gifts; lumps of visceral flesh oozing between his fingers and swollen veins exploding behind an old man's eyes. He had made his blood sacrifice. Oran felt his skin harden and stiffen into platelets like a crustacean's. Smothering the scream that bounced off the walls of his skull until the scream died. He had traded his conscience for a place in history, in a rag-tag army of misfits. Something turned inside Oran, slowly and menacingly, like a stone.

The two of them crossed the bridge. Up ahead a cinema disgorged its audience into the street. A couple of students detached themselves and joined Donie and Oran. As the four made their way towards O'Sheas licensed premises their voices reverberated in the night air and Oran was carried along on the tide of their companionship. He began to feel safe at last. They were all out for a night's drinking, and the rest was as unreal as a bad dream. For the moment, at least, he could convince himself of that.

"I need a pint," Donie said.

Oran tried to visualise how a pint looked and tasted. The cold wet feel of the glass in his hand, the creamy band above the column of black liquid. Even before they arrived at the pub he was savouring its velvety texture as it cascaded into his parched mouth.

But in the smoky golden light of the pub, among the roaring crowd, Oran saw only one man. He would have known those brown baby curls anywhere and he could tell by the way that he leant against the bar and faced into the mirrored wall that Matt Moran was waiting for him.

TWENTY-FIVE

As the car drove away, a silence expanded around her, preparing to swallow her up. The garden stretched out to the band of woodland that encircled the house. Am I so afraid of being alone, she wondered, is that it? The trees creaked, their branches enmeshing in a subtle breeze that danced up from nowhere. Its intrusion was deliberate, like the sound that followed it; the rumble of a car approaching up the driveway. Masked in the trees its arrival was heralded by a hoarse disturbance of crows bursting out of the treetops. They rose and darkened the sky with the black hail of their agitation.

Like a puff of smoke, a cloud drifted across the sun, splitting it into two pink hemispheres. The livid sky infected the landscape below and threw the slated roofs into a sharp unnatural relief. As it disappeared under a canopy of ink-dark cumuli, the sun combusted in a final death-wish.

Facing towards the setting sun, Jane felt light-headed. She was fired by the flamboyance of the sky and the secrets hidden in the dark clouds gathering along the horizon. Her fingers itched with a predatory desire. Close to her shoulder, she could sense a similar hunger to her own and was impatient to reach out to meet it. But instead, she laid her hands decorously in her lap while Mr Heaney took Mrs O'Molloy for an evening drive through the suburbs of Galway. Garret hadn't asked any questions when she had phoned him. Her meeting with Ken and Caroline in the street had filled Jane with a vague terror that had overwhelmed her when she had come home to a silent house and the dirty dishes littering the kitchen table. Feeling like someone drowning, she had reached for the telephone. "I need to see you...I need you."

There had been a pause at the other end of the line and then, in a neutral voice, "Yes."

Pause.

"What time?"

"Nine."

"Where?"

"Here."

His reserve was no surprise. After so long together, both of them were well-versed in the the shorthand of adultery.

Funny, she thought, to visualise them out in the fields like a pair of tinkers. Jane liked the idea of it, the two of them naked in the stubble like animals roaming around in the friendly darkness. No-one could possibly discover them. Safe in the body of night they would become invisible to everyone except to one another. Garret grinned at her out of the dark.

The green light of the dials on the dashboard reflected on his skin, giving his face a strange mask-like quality. "Dining alfresco, tonight, are we?"

She smiled. "Do you think anyone saw us?"

He shrugged without replying. She felt excluded by his silence. She needed him to talk but she hadn't the courage to tell him so. The air was tense with anticipation. All around her, she could feel it swelling up and ready to burst open. Yet here, beside him in the car, she felt utterly alone. It would be different when they could touch each other. Tongues and fingers penetrating the hidden contours of each other's bodies. Along the nerve endings, that's how she and Garret communicated.

Out beyond the last straggling houses at Spiddal, he turned the car off the main road and onto a narrow country road. Through the gathering night they travelled for miles until, at last, a forest spread like a stain across the mountainy landscape. When they came to a clearing Garret stopped the car. He nodded towards a five-bar gate that led into a field. "Come on, this one will do." He was out of the car and half-way across the gate when he paused for her to catch up with him. Hesitantly Jane got out of the car. In the dim light, she could just make out the buckle of his belt swinging. And suddenly, he was moving away from her, an unfamiliar, alien figure, the darkness delineating the distance that he was travelling. Someone she barely knew. Every crease of his body is wonderfully precious to me, she thought, and yet he is so remote I can't even tell if I like him.

"I don't have to do this." The words echoed strangely inside her head like the tolling of a bell. It was a new sound, a new voice that came unbidden out of her mouth. For the first time, Jane saw the scene in which she was a participant. Standing above it as if from a great height, while beneath her, down at the bottom of the pit, she and Garret were preparing to rub up against each other, like dogs in the street. Her feet were weights that she was unable to move, her head a burden that she could barely support.

"What did you say?" He stopped astride the gate. His face was a featureless blank.

"I can't cope with this," she amended her statement. He climbed down immediately. But crouched down, she was ahead of him, arrowing back into the car. In that split second she was conscious of a new intrusion and ducked down to avoid being recognized in the lights of an oncoming car that illuminated the scene. Limbs flying, brain buzzing, she panicked while everything around her was coloured by the terror of being found out. Jesus! He half-toppled in on top of her. She found herself stretched on the floor of the car and beginning to giggle. This is ridiculous! Night closed in again around the departing car and deepening into silence, it smothered any inclination to laughter.

"Get in." Obediently, she climbed out of the back seat and slipped into the passenger seat beside him. A realisation grew, slow and immeasurable. He doesn't care.

He started the car, the gears crashing into place. Even his rage was impenetrable. Cold and contained, like plutonium in a metal casing, clamped into submission by his indomitable will. Among the thoughts crowding her brain she was always conscious of his presence beside her; the inscrutable, fleshy profile that would soon fall away in order that she might come to her deliverance.

"Say something," she asked at last in desperation. Anything was better than these glacial wastes of silence. But even when he spoke, his voice was thin and controlled and venemous.

"It's par for the course," he said. "Just at this moment I'm being carved up on all sides. Cadogan has rigged things good this time. He has the party primed to screw me and the workers down at the plant are extracting my blood. But no-one's going to get to me, I'll make sure of that. No harm in trying though." He was sneering openly at her. "You're only one in a queue, Jane. Everyone's trying to set me up these days."

"Oh, but I didn't set you up." She was shocked at his presumption. Then a suspicion grew in her mind. Could she be sure when she said that? "It wasn't deliberate," she insisted. His face was without expression. As always, she wanted to apologise but now, for once, when she had something to apologise for, the words stuck in her throat. Maybe she wasn't sorry. To have said no, whether with intent or not, that was some kind of achievement.

"Well, whether it was deliberate or not," he said, "you did it."

Yes. On that much they could agree.

Across the dark landscape the sky was still a bright, empurpled colour near the horizon. How strange, Jane thought, at this time of night for there still to be brightness in the sky. And in the east too, how remarkable! It didn't make sense. Everything was extraordinary about this night. The bruised colouring in the sky echoed how she felt inside. If remorse had a colour, she thought, it would be this sore, bluish-crimson shade. As the car drew nearer to the outskirts of Galway, the colour of the sky did not lessen but grew instead and reddened.

In the city the fire had taken hold of the buildings on Nun's Island. Smoke erupted out of the inferno and ascended in great billows but Jane didn't see the flames scud along the edge of the sky nor did she hear the hiss of timber fall.

What had she done? How could she go on without Garret?

TWENTY-SIX

Jane closed the front door. It was a relief to find that she had the house to herself. No sound disturbed the stillness of the darkened rooms. She opened the drawing-room door and leaving the light switched off, she wandered into its shadowy space. A fire was dying in the grate, the last coals flickering listlessly. As she sat down and gazed at the embers, pieces of furniture clustered reassuringly around her like an army of supporters. Everything was in its place. Familiar things that she loved. In the past the thought had often struck her that she would never be totally without worth as long as there was so much stockpiled for her benefit.

Now she had to clear away the superstructure. It was time to strip her life down to the bone and to discover above her head, in the bedrooms, fast asleep under the covers, so much more: the children who threatened to subvert her existence with their absolute trust, and Richard, who never underestimated the distance between them. He too, trusted her. Was this tyranny, as Carol saw it? Sometimes Jane ran away from it, suffocated by it. Sometimes, it paralysed her. A bad complaint! she thought dryly, when there are so many lonely people in the world. If Richard died, or if his love died, the framework would collapse beneath her. People always think that they couldn't go on and yet, they can still make their accommod–ation with death. Widows and widowers, coming to terms with their loss. But Jane had no illusions about the one-sidedness of their compromise. It was like separating plants in autumn, plants whose roots and fibres had so intertwined together over the years that forcing them apart might only destroy them.

Around her the old house shifted in sleep. A window rattled in the wind. A child muttered in a dream. *Mamamamamamama...*

Yes, she answered silently, I'm here.

In the bedroom, Richard would be lying asleep, his head angled into his arm like a young boy. She smiled. We are all so innocent. so slow to learn. We take a lifetime to understand the simplest things. She sat back in the armchair, enjoying the dull warmth escaping from the ashes of the fire.

The sound of the doorbell jolted her out of her reverie. As it echoed through the drawing-room the sound had an angry, peremptory ring. Surely it's not Garret, she thought, returning to do battle. She stood up and patted her hair briskly before going into the hall. Don't be idiotic, she told herself.

The sight of Oran Reidy standing on the step caused her to step back in surprise. Her first reaction was to wonder if she had remembered to pay him his wages.

And then, looking closely at him, she realized how white and pinched and alert his face was. He looked like an animal about to attack. She cringed involuntarily. Blackmail, was that it? She had often wondered how she would respond to a threat. We have proof, Mrs O'Molloy, would you like to take a look for yourself, or perhaps your husband would prefer to see these photographs? But Oran Reidy didn't seem interested in showing her any photographs. Without speaking, he continued to watch her closely, his foot on the step as if he were about to leap past her into the house. They stared at each other. Both of them were on their guard, waiting to see who would make the first move. "I need to hide..." His voice faltered.

Relief surged through her. So, she thought, here was someone else who felt it too! She straightened up and examined him with a dispassionate curiosity. He could have been Garret. He had the same neat head and roughened hands. A slimmed-down version of the real thing. A Garret who was twenty years younger and who had not yet skidded plumply into middle-age. The boy even had the same impenetrable expression in his eyes. She felt a stab of pain; a pelvic gnaw that started up without warning. She knew what to expect from now on. Already she was preparing for the moment when her eyes flicked awake at the beginning of each day, and the spruce, pinstripe-suited phantom of Garret Heaney would be waiting for her.

She felt the pain then, so acutely that tears sprang in her eyes. Hallucinations, she would inform her other self, the one that grovelled, bereft and howling. Withdrawal symptoms. When I've cracked this one, she would continue, cold and unrelenting and reaching out to the bedside table for a cigarette, then I'll give up the ciggies.

Funny how she had never noticed the resemblance before. Maybe there wasn't any, she thought tiredly, maybe all men look the same in the dark. She smiled at Oran. So here we stand, she thought, both of us living in terror of being found out. "Just give me the key to the studio," he said. She had hired him, she remembered, to build her the studio. And now the work was almost complete; the partitions cleared away, windows were in, and the floor laid. That beautiful white deal floor. Now that it was finished, the whole business had turned out to be a meaningless exercise. What had been constructed was nothing more than an elaborate housing designed to accommodate a non-existent machine. A machine that had no form, and no substance.

So what did she believe in? On the beach the boy had posed that question. And the only response he had received had been the lament of seabirds, drifting up the windless air. Now she was in a position to answer his question. She didn't believe in any of his sentimental savagery, that was for sure. And she didn't share in the conviction that had her sister running away with the fairies. Carol believed in the future and Oran believed in the past. As for Jane, she no longer believed in the present. She knew what she was not and that surely, was some kind of progress. Put not your trust in pricks. That was something she believed in, for a start. And there was something else she knew now. She knew where she belonged. Her hunger for Garret might never go away. She would just have to take that chance. As it was, it seeped up through faults in the structure when she was least able to cope. Drunk particularly, she would feel it crawl along the surface of her skin. But she was able for it now. One day at a time, Sweet Jeezus, that's all I'm asking...

She caught her reflection in a mirror. So why aren't you smiling, she asked the silent woman who watched her from a distance across the glass.

Jane undid the clasp of her handbag. Handbag rummaging was an activity acceptable in a woman. Oh my, she thought, there I go again, looking for approbation. I'm a good girl really. A nice girl, like Mama always wanted me to be. See what I did to Mr Heaney and his nasty big thing when he stood at the five-bar gate? Mother Stan and the nuns of Claraville would have been proud of me. Metaphorically speaking, I cut it down to size tonight. And now here you are, looking for help. Young man, don't you know the kind of woman you're dealing with?

"No," she said, enchanted by the new authority of

her refusal. She felt sorry for Oran and would have liked to have offered him an explanation but she couldn't afford to deviate from the course mapped out for her. It was so fragile, the life she was constructing for herself, so susceptible to upset.

"No," she said more gently, "I couldn't possibly. Now, please..."

As she was shutting the door she found what she was looking for. She took it out and carefully closed the clasp of her bag. Then, before the door closed on him completely, she stretched out her hand to give it to Oran.

As soon as Jane opened the front door, Oran realised his mistake. Up until that moment he had convinced himself that he would be safe there. All the way out to Bearna he had envisaged the gate into the yard swinging open to receive him. There was no doubt in his mind. In that ruined enclosure he would find sanctuary. It had sustained him, the vision of the studio, shining like a beacon, and so proximate that his imagination had already burrowed a way through. The scent of cut timber was alive in his nostrils and he saw himself huddled down in the shadows and able to gaze at the moonlight, delicate and unsullied, as it dipped through the dormer windows.

When he had arrived at the entrance gates, the gravel on the driveway crunched familiarly under his feet. An owl hooted in the trees. Framed by the avenue of trees—the way he had visualised it—the courtyard wall was like a rampart in which the gate was a dark baleful eye. When he was close enough to stretch out his hand to grasp the latch at last, he felt light-headed with triumph.

Not caught yet!

But, resolute on its hinges, the gate thwarted him. It refused to budge. Even when he pushed hard against it, the bolts offered him nothing but resistance. He couldn't believe it. The freedom to hide was all that was left to him and he wasn't ready to give it up. While a place of his salvation existed, clear and defined and sharpened into focus, he wouldn't give it up, not as long as the secret enclave tugged at him with the compulsion of home.

A gust of wind chased up the driveway, chivvying the trees into a frenzy. A recklessness took root, a crazy instinct to gamble everything he had on Jane O'Molloy. Among Oran's inchoate thoughts, there grew a conviction about how the world was put together and about the collusion between Jane O'Molloy and Garret Heaney. All of them, their caste— and he still felt sick at the thought—had won a victory tonight and they owed him. Tonight Mrs Jane O'Molloy could afford to be generous. Oran stepped back from the locked gate and let his gaze travel over the façade of the house. The upstairs windows were shuttered for the night but around the front door, a band of light escaped. It was the only indication of her presence and yet, he knew that Jane O'Molloy was somewhere, beyond the door. Waiting for him.

As he wavered on the steps the shadows deepened dangerously around him. Night in the countryside... he could never get accustomed to its absolute blackness. In his ears his breath thundered, loud and uncomfortable. He swallowed and the thunder lessened. He touched the doorbell and it responded immediately. A deep, muted voice. In the silence that followed the dying ring of the bell Oran felt his certainty unravel. Exhausted, he leant against the door-jamb, trying to quell the fear erupting inside him. All his life he had hungered for doors to open, had waited on the threshold for some revelation, some direction to follow, some imperative to obey. In that moment he forgot that it was Jane O'Molloy that he was waiting for, and he forgot his vision of the studio across the yard. All he remembered was the need, the habitual yearning, and at the core of desire, only despair.

It was so predictable—the opening door, the sudden luminescence as she switched on the hall-light, the gilt and tawny-coloured carpet. A glimpse through an inner door, that had been left ajar, revealed polished mahogany, gold-patterned plates, lace and silver candlesticks sprouting fat rosy candles. How could he have possibly thought that it would be otherwise?

Her face had an unearthly look about it. Her mouth was razor-outlined in carmine and her eyes were abnormally large and fringed with spiky lashes that were coated with mascara. He wondered at how alien she looked, he who had seen beneath her clothes and had seen her limbs, delicate and white, wading into water.

"Yes?" she asked, her hand rubbing nervously along the belt of her dress.

He began to speak. "Just give me a chance. I'll leave you alone...I will." And then he stopped. It was madness to explain. In his voice he could hear an old desperation. Voices of women flowed in to merge with his. Out of his past they came wheedling for favours. Ah give us a chance. Next week I'll have it, so I will. Just once more, and I'll have it for you, so I will...And like a distant bell, the mute appeal of Dominick's wife found articulation. Help me, help me, help me...

Oran was exhausted, barely able to control the shaking in his legs. "I need to hide," he said. She looked at him blankly. "Just give me the key to the studio." It was hopeless.

Momentarily her glance shifted past him, into the night-filled garden as if checking to make sure that there were no more like Oran, out on the lawn and clamouring to be let in. The rich must live like this always, he thought, the spectre of revolt forever lurking in the recesses of their minds. Theirs was a private folk-memory of the dispossessed gathering up to challenge their authority.

The risen people.

Yes. There was no doubt about it, she was reassured by his solitariness. Jane O'Molloy almost smiled at him. There was a twinkling somewhere, in her eyes, that had him figuring in a good after-dinner story, maybe, or in some future pillow-talk.

"No," she said crisply.

High above their heads, a wind leapt up through the trees, clattering branches together. She shuddered in the cold draught and pulled her cardigan closer around her shoulders. "I couldn't possibly," she said. She bent her head and rummaged in her handbag. An emptiness washed over Oran. In his confusion he sought for an explanation. That there had to be death and destruction for all this, for the protection of these high windows and long lawns and silverware piled up on the sideboard and for the power that underpinned them...Oran couldn't begin to put his thoughts in order. Images clustered like an army regrouping in retreat; of Dominick and MacIntyre and Garret Heaney conspiring to lay waste a generation; and Fergus beating at the flames that had been kindled to destroy his dreams. And in the heart of the fire, an old man butchered by a schoolboy. Who could rise against the likes of them?

Jane O'Molloy raised her head and faced him. As she spoke her face was expressionless. "Here, take this." He wanted to make a stand, to say something. Anything. But he was powerless, unable to say a word. "And now," she said quietly, "please go away."

How polite she was to the very end! The door slid across his face and closed in the warmth, the shimmering lights, the aromatic air. In the dark, Oran stood on the step and looked down at what she had handed him before she closed the door.

In the palm of his hand was a crumpled five-pound note.

TWENTY-SEVEN

Night landed in around him with the weight of a blanket falling over his eyes. Uncertainly he began to retrace his steps along the driveway. In his confusion, he lost his way and stumbled among the trees. As he lurched around in the dark, stray branches whipped across his cheeks and along the ground, brambles clutched at his ankles. Disoriented, he felt the anchors slip.

Christ, he was adrift.

No way forward, no way back. He could have been anywhere, it made no difference. There was no place for him in the vacuum that had been burnt out by events. The murky hollowness that enveloped him, smelt of cinders and he was frightened of the spectres rising up to surround him. Where am I, he wanted to cry as he crashed around senselessly in the undergrowth. Even the expectation of Matt Moran landing him was bearable in comparison to this new terror.

Without warning, the tilting world righted itself. Beyond the gates the road was suddenly revealed, its surface glinting with a strange luminosity while, high in the sky, a new moon, like a pale incandescent vessel, emerged from behind the banks of cloud. But the light it offered was a lustre without life, a cadaverous gleam. So here I go forward, he urged himself and his legs responded mechanically to his call, thudding along the tarmac to a rhythm of their own making.